A BLUEPRINT FOR BELONGING

BUILDING A POSITIVE
SCHOOL CULTURE
FROM THE GROUND UP

MORGANE MICHAEL

Solution Tree | Press

Copyright © 2024 by Solution Tree Press

Materials appearing here are copyrighted. With one exception, all rights are reserved. Readers may reproduce only those pages marked "Reproducible." Otherwise, no part of this book may be reproduced or transmitted in any form or by any means (electronic, photocopying, recording, or otherwise) without prior written permission of the publisher.

Cover images created with AI-assisted Adobe Stock images.

555 North Morton Street
Bloomington, IN 47404
800.733.6786 (toll free) / 812.336.7700
FAX: 812.336.7790

email: info@SolutionTree.com
SolutionTree.com

Visit **go.SolutionTree.com/SEL** to download the free reproducibles in this book.

Printed in the United States of America

Library of Congress Cataloging-in-Publication Data

Names: Michael, Morgane, author.
Title: A blueprint for belonging : building a positive school culture from
   the ground up / Morgane Michael.
Description: Bloomington, IN : Solution Tree Press, 2024. | Includes
   bibliographical references and index.
Identifiers: LCCN 2024003789 (print) | LCCN 2024003790 (ebook) | ISBN
   9781960574466 (paperback) | ISBN 9781960574473 (ebook)
Subjects: LCSH: School environment. | Motivation in education. | Academic
   achievement--Psychological aspects.
Classification: LCC LC210 .M54 2024 (print) | LCC LC210 (ebook) | DDC
   371--dc23/eng/20240228
LC record available at https://lccn.loc.gov/2024003789
LC ebook record available at https://lccn.loc.gov/2024003790

_____

Solution Tree
Jeffrey C. Jones, CEO
Edmund M. Ackerman, President

Solution Tree Press
President and Publisher: Douglas M. Rife
Associate Publishers: Todd Brakke and Kendra Slayton
Editorial Director: Laurel Hecker
Art Director: Rian Anderson
Copy Chief: Jessi Finn
Senior Production Editor: Christine Hood
Copy Editor: Mark Hain
Proofreader: Sarah Ludwig
Cover Designer: Rian Anderson
Acquisitions Editors: Carol Collins and Hilary Goff
Assistant Acquisitions Editor: Elijah Oates
Content Development Specialist: Amy Rubenstein
Associate Editor: Sarah Ludwig
Editorial Assistant: Anne Marie Watkins

ACKNOWLEDGMENTS

I would like to express my gratitude to all the people who not only believed in the vision I had for this book, but also supported my speaking efforts and coaching, took chances on my vision, and gave me meaningful feedback that pushed this work (and me) to be better. Feedback is a gift!

Specifically, thank you to my children, Makena and Tyson, who teach, inspire, and cheer me on daily. Thank you to my family, who has always jumped up with enthusiasm to celebrate the wins (especially Kathy, Lynn, Mom, and Kelly). Thank you to my girlfriends, my chosen family, who consistently show up for me (Jodie, Laura, Carly, Chloe, Megan, Deanne, Bianca, Kim, Heather, Kathleen, Lisa, Lauren, and Trish). Thank you, Josh, for encouraging, pushing, and believing in me.

Solution Tree Press would like to thank the following reviewers:

John D. Ewald
Education Consultant
Frederick, Maryland

Ian Landy
District Principal of Technology
School District 47
Powell River, British Columbia, Canada

Katie Saunders
Elementary/Middle School Teacher
Anglophone School District West
Fredericton, New Brunswick, Canada

John Unger
Principal
West Fork Middle School
West Fork, Arkansas

Sheryl Walters
Senior School Assistant Principal
Calgary, Alberta, Canada

Allison Zamarripa
Literacy Instructional Specialist
Pasadena Independent School District
Pasadena, Texas

Visit **go.SolutionTree.com/SEL** to download the free reproducibles in this book.

TABLE OF CONTENTS

Reproducibles are in italics.

About the Author .... **vii**

Introduction **1**
   Belonging in Schools: More Important Than Ever 5
   Challenges of Building a Belonging Culture in Schools 7
   Belonging for Adults 10
   In This Book 11

Chapter 1
The Foundation: Building a Culture of Belonging **15**
   A Focus on Belonging to Yourself First 18
   Five Strategies for Building Belonging as Educators and School Leaders 19
   Belonging in Schools 22
   Classroom Toolbox 24
   School Leadership Toolbox 30
   Conclusion 36
   Designing Your Blueprint: Laying the Foundation for Belonging 38

Chapter 2
A Positive School Culture: Fostering Generosity, Kindness, and Empathy **39**
   Kindness as a Priority 42
   Giving Styles 45
   The Recognition Gap 48
   The Contagion of Incivility in Schools 51
   Belonging Through Proximity 53

Belonging Cues...55
The Vulnerability Cycle...56
Classroom Toolbox...59
School Leadership Toolbox...70
Conclusion...76
Designing Your Blueprint: Using Kindness as a Building Block...77

Chapter 3

Bias Exploration: Dismantling Implicit Bias in Schools...79

Definitions of Equity, Diversity, and Inclusion Within the Context of Bias...82
The Meaning of Bias...85
A Reveal of the Unseen...87
A Safe Environment for All...88
Case Studies of Inclusive and Diverse Schools...91
Classroom Toolbox...97
School Leadership Toolbox...109
Conclusion...117
Designing Your Blueprint: Addressing Implicit Bias in Schools...118

Chapter 4

Restorative Justice: Repairing Harm and Building Relationships...119

The Meaning of Restorative Justice...121
Core Principles of Restorative Justice...123
Obstacles to Restorative Justice Practices...128
Evaluation and Continuous Improvement of Restorative Justice Practices...130
Classroom Toolbox...131
School Leadership Toolbox...142
Conclusion...146
Designing Your Blueprint: Restorative Justice and Building Relationships...147

Epilogue...149

References and Resources...151

Index...163

ABOUT THE AUTHOR

Morgane Michael has been an elementary school educator with the Greater Victoria School District in British Columbia, Canada, since 2008. Morgane is a passionate advocate for social-emotional learning, kindness education, and educator well-being, and she leads professional development initiatives aligned with those efforts throughout her province.

Morgane has pursued her interest in developing positive school culture through kindness and self-compassion practices, promoting effective social collaboration, nurturing creativity, and building self-efficacy that is responsive to students' needs. She established a culture of high expectations by launching her podcast, *KindSight 101*, in 2018. She has interviewed some of the world's biggest names in education on the topics of kindness, well-being, self-compassion, and promoting positive school culture. Morgane is also the creator and founder of the Small Act Big Impact 21-Day Kindness Challenge, which seeks to promote and cultivate safe and supportive school culture. She shares insights from her podcast and lesson ideas on her blog, *Small Act, Big Impact* (www.morganemichael.com).

As a speaker and personal performance coach, Morgane has had the pleasure of helping thousands of educators crush their personal and professional goals through powerful lifestyle changes, impactful mindset shifts, and massive action commitments to create a compelling, purpose-filled future.

Morgane received a bachelor's degree in elementary education from the University of Victoria, British Columbia, as well as a master's degree in educational leadership. She lives with her family in Victoria, British Columbia.

To learn more about Morgane Michael's work, visit her website and blog (www.morganemichael.com); follow her at smallactbigimpact on Instagram, at Morgane Michael Consulting on Facebook, or @MorganeMichael on X (formerly Twitter); or listen to her *KindSight 101* podcast.

To book Morgane Michael for professional development, contact pd@SolutionTree.com.

INTRODUCTION

It was 2011 when Sara Martinez faced what seemed to be an impossible challenge. As a top-performing principal, she had been tasked with merging three Title I high schools serving low-income communities, each burdened with decreasing enrollment and a crippling reputation for violence.

Sara understood the struggles these students faced because she had faced them too, growing up in poverty herself. Fueled by a determination to create change and informed by her own experiences as a student in the California school system, she pursued leadership roles, eventually rising as a principal.

The very first day, Sara knew it was time to take charge. Against the warnings of faculty, Sara gathered all the students in the auditorium to introduce herself and set the tone for the new chapter of their educational journey together. The chaos that ensued was remarkable. Students were running in from all directions. The noise slowly subsided as curious eyes turned toward their new leader. As Sara began addressing the students, acknowledging their roles, responsibilities, and identities as scholars within the school, a student at the back of the room caught Sara's attention. The student stood up and asked, "You call this a school?"

In that moment, Sara realized the underlying issue: these students didn't see their school as a place of learning or belonging. They saw it as a place of limits and constraints, with abandoned bulletin boards, overwhelmed teachers, unruly students, and classrooms cluttered with trash and neglected materials. Neither the school nor the students felt worthy of anything better.

"Can I really do this?" she wondered, trying to recover from the initial shock. "The state of this school is so disheartening." In that moment, it became Sara's mission to transform the school.

Sara became a fanatic about bulletin boards and putting up positive quotes in the hallways, stressing the importance of positive messaging and telling students every day why they were special. No detail was overlooked as the faculty cleaned classrooms, replaced broken furniture, and brightened the halls with vibrant colors. The chains that once bound the front doors were removed, symbolizing a new era of hope and opportunity. Sara led a team in redesigning the school budget, reallocating funds to hire more teachers and support staff, and reconstructing the daily schedule to offer a diverse range of educational opportunities. Professional development became a cornerstone of change, equipping teachers with the necessary tools to cater to the diverse needs of their students. They implemented a lesson-delivery model focused on small-group instruction, ensuring every student's individual needs were met.

But it wasn't just about the physical changes; it was about shifting mindsets and eliminating excuses. Sara and her staff analyzed the prevailing challenges, biases, and deeply entrenched trauma, and committed to overcoming them together through training and restorative practices.

Sara recognized the importance of addressing the underlying issues that led to negative and self-destructive behaviors. She approached the teachers, asking them, "What are we missing? What clues and signals did we overlook?" She urged the staff to pay attention, question, and acknowledge their realities. It was not just about disciplining students; it was about recognizing their pain, offering support, and guiding them toward a better path. The conversation shifted from blame to compassion, from frustration to determination.

Over the morning announcements, Sara reminded students of the school's core values: focus, tradition, excellence, integrity, and perseverance. She emphasized how education has the power to transform their lives and open doors they never thought possible.

Eventually, test scores improved, surpassing all expectations. The school, students, and faculty defied the odds, proving that change is possible when we eliminate excuses and commit to excellence.

Sara's impact extended far beyond the walls of the school. Her remarkable story of perseverance and success garnered national attention, inspiring educators, policymakers, and individuals from all walks of life. Through her story, Sara is an example of the incredible impact one person can make when driven by a profound belief in the potential of every student.

In this book, *A Blueprint for Belonging*, you will delve deep into the essence of what makes a school. An excellent school is not simply a place of learning, but a place built on the concept of home, where belonging and identity converge (Allen, Kern,

Vella-Brodrick, Hattie, & Waters, 2018). Fostering a sense of home is what Sara Martinez created through relentless perseverance, heart, and human connection. Belonging can serve as the cornerstone for fostering a vibrant community within our schools (Allen, Waters, Arslan, & Prentice, 2022).

Sara's story demonstrates how transformative the power of empathy, the strength found in unity, and the profound impact of believing in the potential of each student can be in co-constructing a school that changes lives. By weaving together practical strategies with heartwarming insights, this book aims to inspire educators, paraprofessionals, and school leaders alike to cultivate an environment where every individual feels valued, understood, and connected. In doing so, you not only enhance morale and cohesion but also empower students to thrive in a world that values diversity and inclusivity.

When I use the term *leader* in this book, I'm not just referring to those in traditional positions of power. I acknowledge the leadership embodied by teachers and paraprofessionals. Leadership is not about titles; it's a conscious choice to inspire, guide, and uplift. Every day, educators make the deliberate choice to lead, shaping minds and futures far beyond classroom walls.

The intersection of leadership and personal ownership over your environment plays a pivotal role in shaping a culture of belonging—a principle that resonates deeply with me both professionally and personally. The environment you create and navigate is not just happenstance but the result of conscious choices and actions (Allen et al., 2018). Everyone has the power to influence their surroundings positively, fostering spaces where all feel included and valued.

Reflecting on my own journey, I think back to my time as an immigrant from France—a time marked by a feeling of overwhelming isolation and a desire to belong, at all costs, and a willingness to compromise elements of my own identity to do so. In many ways, this experience has guided my dedication to fostering true inclusion in every school. This narrative is not just mine but echoes the experiences of countless individuals who've had similar experiences of compromising who they are to gain a sense of belonging.

During my years as a student who moved to small, rural, artsy Gabriola Island in British Columbia, Canada, at the age of four, I often felt like an outsider, detached from the norms that seemed to easily define others. Growing up, French was my first language. For many, speaking French might seem interesting or even exotic. But for me, in an environment where English dominated, it often felt like a spotlight highlighting my differences. I picked up English mainly through my school, trying my best to fit in.

I distinctly remember a time in second grade when I decided to stop speaking French at home. It was a conscious effort to blend in, to not feel so "other." Now, as an adult, I see the beauty and value in my bilingual upbringing. I've even spent a decade teaching in French immersion programs. But that journey from feeling out of place to embracing my unique background wasn't easy. It's a testament to the complexities of identity and the human desire to belong.

Post-COVID, I recognize this same yearning for belonging in many around me. The world is changing, and our places within it seem uncertain. As an educator and leader, I believe it's my duty to guide and foster environments of inclusivity where students feel free to show up fully as themselves. This book is my endeavor to provide insights and tools for all those seeking to cultivate spaces of belonging, both for themselves and others. As leaders and educators, our responsibilities go beyond just imparting knowledge. They include nurturing, guiding, and creating environments where every individual feels seen, heard, and most importantly, a sense of belonging.

Creating a school culture of inclusion, belonging, and positivity requires a carefully crafted blueprint, much like a builder's blueprint for constructing a house. Educators and school leaders should approach the task of constructing a positive and inclusive school culture with the same level of planning, precision, and attention to detail as a builder constructing a sturdy and beautiful home. To achieve this, they should equip themselves with a toolbox filled with various strategies designed to promote belonging and foster positivity.

Just as a builder selects the right tools for the job, educators and school leaders must carefully select and implement the right strategy for each situation, ensuring they are building a culture that is strong, resilient, and lasting. With the proper blueprint and toolbox of strategies, educators and school leaders can construct a school culture that is welcoming and inclusive, and fosters a sense of belonging for all students, providing a strong foundation for their academic and personal success. So, if you're ready to take your school culture to the next level, let's dive in!

This introduction explores ten key research-based reasons why creating a culture of belonging is essential for the well-being and achievement of both students and educators. These insights reveal how belonging significantly affects academic outcomes, emotional strength, and the school atmosphere. We also examine roadblocks in creating such a culture, including implicit bias, the need for culturally responsive practices, communication issues, and the complexities of power and privilege.

This chapter also introduces the BUILD framework—boundaries, understanding, integrity, listening, and dependability—as a guide for creating inclusive educational spaces. The BUILD framework offers educators actionable strategies to ensure every school member feels valued and connected. My intent is that readers will understand the vital importance of belonging in schools and be ready to implement strategies for a more inclusive and supportive educational environment.

Belonging in Schools: More Important Than Ever

Many students, teachers, and school leaders do not feel like they belong in their schools, and educators and leaders sometimes find themselves at a loss as how to foster a sense of belonging in their classrooms and schools. Students from marginalized backgrounds are at particular risk of feeling disconnected and unsupported (Allen et al., 2022). The pandemic has only exacerbated these challenges, making it even more important to prioritize belonging in our schools.

In our ever-changing world, schools should be more than just academic institutions. They should also be places where students feel like they belong, where they can thrive emotionally and socially as well as academically. By creating a culture of belonging, you can foster a more positive, supportive, and inclusive educational environment that benefits everyone. This book is for anyone who is committed to creating a better future for students and their communities, especially in the wake of the pandemic's impact on connection and community.

Research shows that a sense of belonging is crucial for students' academic success, social-emotional development, and overall well-being (Afsar & Umrani, 2020; Gaete, Rojas-Barahona, Olivares, & Araya, 2016). While culture is essential, one might argue that focusing too much on culture can take away from academic rigor and achievement. Others might suggest that by prioritizing culture over academics, schools could be lowering the bar for student achievement and not adequately preparing students for the real world. Additionally, some people believe that culture and belonging initiatives can be costly, and schools may not have the resources to allocate to these programs, or that culture-building initiatives can be difficult to implement and sustain, especially in schools with high staff turnover rates. However, as noted in the following text, research shows quite the opposite!

When students feel like they belong, they are more engaged in their learning, have higher self-esteem, and are less likely to experience mental health problems (Walton & Cohen, 2011). Similarly, teachers and school leaders who feel like they belong are more effective in their roles, have higher job satisfaction, and are more likely to stay in their positions long term (Rivera, 2024).

Belonging is a fundamental human need and is crucial for healthy development, particularly in school-aged children (Rivera, 2024). The following are ten research-based reasons why belonging helps students in school.

1. **Positive academic outcomes:** A sense of belonging in school is linked to better academic achievement, engagement, and lower dropout rates (Allen et al., 2018; Gaete et al., 2016; Osterman, 2000).

2. **Better mental health:** Students who feel like they belong in school experience lower levels of anxiety, depression, and stress. They also have higher self-esteem and a more positive sense of identity (Allen et al., 2018; Osterman, 2000; Walton & Cohen, 2011).

3. **Increased motivation:** A sense of belonging is linked to higher levels of motivation, goal setting, and achievement (Furrer & Skinner, 2003; Osterman, 2000).

4. **Improved social skills:** Students who feel like they belong are better able to form positive relationships with peers and adults. They are also more likely to exhibit prosocial behaviors, such as kindness, empathy, and compassion (Allen et al., 2018; Osterman, 2000; Walton & Cohen, 2011).

5. **Reduced bullying and aggression:** When students feel like they belong, they are less likely to engage in bullying and aggressive behaviors. They are also less likely to be victimized by these behaviors (Gaete et al., 2016; Osterman, 2000).

6. **Higher attendance:** Students who feel like they belong in school are more likely to attend regularly and participate in school activities (Allen et al., 2018; Osterman, 2000).

7. **Better school climate:** A positive school culture results when students feel like they belong. This, in turn, leads to a more supportive and inclusive learning environment for all students (Allen et al., 2018; Gaete et al., 2016; Walton & Cohen, 2011).

8. **Improved parental involvement:** When students feel like they belong in school, their parents are more likely to be involved in their education and school activities (Allen et al., 2018; Gaete et al., 2016).

9. **Increased resilience:** Students who feel like they belong in school are more resilient and better able to cope with challenges and setbacks (Allen et al., 2018; Osterman, 2000).

10. **Long-term benefits:** A sense of belonging in school is linked to positive outcomes later in life, including higher educational attainment, better employment outcomes, and improved mental health (Allen et al., 2018; Walton & Cohen, 2011).

In exploring the concept of belonging and its critical role in shaping individual and community well-being, it is important to understand the role of isolation. Despite being surrounded by others, you can still feel profoundly alone until you discover spaces where your interests and identities are not just accepted but celebrated (Giroux, 2021). As you read Luke's story, think about the value of community and the power of finding one's place within it, highlighting the collective journey toward a more empathetic and connected society.

> Luke was raised in the heart of a big American city. With the constant buzz and hum of urban life, he often felt like an outsider. Although surrounded by people, he felt isolated, believing that no one could truly see or understand him. One day, while passing a local community center, Luke was enticed in by the sound of drums. Drawn to the beat, he discovered a music group practicing for an upcoming performance. Hesitant at first, he was eventually encouraged to join in. This became his refuge—a place where his love for drums was not just recognized but celebrated. He joined the band at his high school and found friends who were just as passionate as he.

Challenges of Building a Belonging Culture in Schools

Creating a culture of belonging in schools involves addressing challenges such as implicit bias and stereotype threat, implementing culturally responsive practices, promoting effective communication and collaboration, and tackling issues of power and privilege (Newkirk, 2019). Within this book, we will explore all four challenges and offer some meaningful and effective strategies to address them to build dynamic school cultures.

Implicit Bias and Stereotype Threats

One of the most significant challenges is the presence of implicit bias and stereotype threats. *Implicit bias* refers to unconscious attitudes or stereotypes that influence our perceptions and interactions with others. *Stereotype threats* occur when individuals feel at risk of confirming a negative stereotype about their group, which can lead to anxiety and underperformance (Johnson, Alvarez, Hughes, McQuade, & Fuentes, 2024). For example, a study by Steven J. Spencer, Christine Logel, and Paul G. Davies (2016) finds that simply reminding female college students of their gender before a mathematics test can trigger stereotype threat, leading to lower performance compared to when no reminder is given. Female students may underperform on mathematics tests due to the pervasive stereotype that males are better at mathematics.

In another example, African American and Latino students often face stereotype threats related to assumptions about their academic abilities. Research by Gregory M. Walton and Geoffrey L. Cohen (2011) shows that interventions designed to mitigate feelings of uncertainly about social belonging in college could significantly improve the grades of African American students.

Culturally Responsive Practices

Another roadblock to building belonging in schools is the need for culturally responsive practices. *Culturally responsive practices* involve recognizing and valuing the cultural backgrounds and experiences of all students and incorporating them into the curriculum and classroom environment (Gay, 2018). For example, a study of an elementary school with a large Hispanic population found that when teachers incorporated culturally responsive practices into their instruction, students reported feeling more connected to the school and had higher levels of academic achievement (Rivera, 2024). The following scenario illustrates how culturally responsive practices can help students from all backgrounds and experiences.

> Being a first-generation immigrant, Elijah was acutely aware of the differences between his family's traditions and those of his peers. Birthday celebrations, food, and even weekend activities felt different from what his middle school classmates shared. Elijah's social studies teacher, recognizing his unique perspective, asked him to present a family tradition to the class. This led to the formation of an international club at school where students celebrated global festivals and learned about diverse cultures. Elijah no longer felt different; he felt valued.

Taking time to acknowledge and celebrate differences can make a tremendous difference in the way students feel.

Effective Communication

Another difficulty many schools face when setting out to create a culture of belonging is the lack of effective communication and collaboration between teachers, students, and families. Effective communication and collaboration require creating opportunities for dialogue and feedback, as well as involving families and community members in school decision making (Jaiswal & Prasad, 2020). It is common for stakeholders to have a difficult time communicating clearly to foster a common set of priorities and values. In one study, researchers found that when teachers at a middle school with a predominantly African American student population collaborated with families and community members more actively, students reported feeling more connected to their school and had higher levels of academic achievement (Jaiswal & Prasad, 2020).

Integrating students with exceptional or priority needs into the school culture is vital for fostering inclusion. The story of Zara, a student with a hearing impairment, exemplifies the importance of leveraging individual strengths to enhance belonging.

> Born with a hearing impairment, Zara felt isolated in group discussions, but she could always be found sketching, doodling, and escaping through art. Her art teacher observed her passion and introduced her to a mural project for the school. As students collaborated on the mural, they were able to connect through their love for art and found a way to communicate with Zara through gestures; some even learned sign language.

Sometimes, it takes a special educator to see the need for collaboration and create the opportunity for students to engage with one another effectively.

Power and Privilege

Many educational institutions are revisiting and exploring issues of power and privilege because of significant global and political events related to race and diversity (Newkirk, 2019). Addressing issues of power and privilege involves examining and challenging systems and practices that perpetuate inequities and marginalization (Bradshaw, 2018; Newkirk, 2019). Education scholar Geneva Gay (2018) argues that culturally responsive teaching and addressing power and privilege can increase students' academic achievement, self-efficacy, and engagement by validating and incorporating their cultural identities into the classroom.

As educational institutions navigate the complexities of power, privilege, and diversity, it becomes increasingly clear that the conversation cannot stop with student experiences alone. The same principles of inclusion and belonging for creating supportive environments for students also hold value for adults within the school system (Afsar & Umrani, 2020; Allen et al., 2018).

Belonging for Adults

It is essential not only to focus on the well-being and psychological safety of students, but also to extend that focus on belonging to the adults in the building. The following are five research-based reasons for focusing on the overall workplace culture of a school, including adults.

1. **Improved educator well-being and job satisfaction:** A psychologically safe and inclusive workplace culture can enhance employees' sense of well-being and job satisfaction, leading to improved performance and reduced turnover (Afsar & Umrani, 2020).

2. **Enhanced creativity and innovation:** Psychological safety and a sense of belonging can encourage employees to feel comfortable taking risks, sharing new ideas, and engaging in creative problem solving, which can lead to increased innovation and productivity (Carmeli & Gittell, 2009).

3. **Increased teamwork and collaboration:** A psychologically safe and inclusive workplace culture can foster positive relationships between colleagues and increase collaboration, which can lead to better teamwork and improved organizational outcomes (Edmondson, 2019).

4. **Better decision making:** A culture of psychological safety and belonging can encourage open and honest communication, allowing for better decision making and problem solving within teams and organizations (Detert & Edmondson, 2011).

5. **Higher performance:** Organizations with a positive culture of psychological safety and belonging tend to outperform those without such a culture in terms of financial and achievement-related outcomes (De Smet, Rubenstein, Schrah, Vierow, & Edmondson, 2021).

In This Book

As the world continues to grapple with the effects of the COVID-19 pandemic, it's clear that schools are still contending with its impact on education (Allen et al., 2022; Chellathurai, 2020). The pandemic has created unprecedented challenges for students, teachers, and school leaders, from social isolation to increased stress and anxiety (Chellathurai, 2020). Now more than ever, it is critical to create a school environment in which everyone feels valued, included, and supported.

This book provides evidence-based strategies for creating a culture of belonging in schools, including ways to address challenges and obstacles you might face. Each chapter focuses on a different aspect of belonging, including creating a foundation for belonging; fostering kindness, generosity, and positivity; exploring bias exploration; and implementing restorative justice practices. Drawing on the latest research and practical, actionable examples from a variety of schools, this book provides a road map for fostering a sense of belonging for all members of the school community.

Chapter 1 lays the foundation for understanding just how critical belonging is to mental health, academic achievement, and an overall sense of fulfillment. In their meta-analysis of belonging in schools, Kelly-Ann Allen, Margaret Kern, Dianne Vella-Brodrick, John Hattie, and Lea Waters (2018) find that students who feel like they belong are more likely to achieve higher grades, experience better mental health outcomes, and engage in fewer risky behaviors.

Chapter 2 explores the power of kindness and generosity in building a culture of belonging. It examines the power of positivity in creating a culture of belonging and provides practical strategies for promoting positivity in your school community, from practicing gratitude to celebrating successes to practicing empathy. It also discusses how to incorporate kindness into daily school life to create a more positive and supportive environment, as well as the importance of generosity in fostering connections and building a sense of belonging in classrooms and the workplace. It includes real-world examples and actionable tips for creating a more generous school community.

Chapter 3 highlights the crucial role of bias exploration in creating a truly inclusive school community. It offers actionable strategies for recognizing and addressing biases and promoting equity and inclusion in the classroom and beyond.

Finally, chapter 4 focuses on the principles of restorative justice and their role in building a positive and supportive school culture. Through the latest research and practical advice, it explores how implementing restorative practices can transform a school's culture.

Building a culture of belonging and an inclusive culture in schools is like constructing a structure from the ground up. Just as a building can't stand without a strong frame, a school can't succeed without a strong community of teachers, students, and parents. It's essential to use the right materials and techniques to make sure the structure is strong and long lasting. To ensure you have the right materials and tools to build this culture, each chapter also features a Classroom Toolbox and School Leadership Toolbox of engaging activities, which highlight the following five BUILD belonging elements: boundaries, understanding, integrity, listening, and dependability.

- **B—Boundaries:** Just as a building needs a strong foundation, a culture of belonging requires clear boundaries and guidelines (Sullivan, 2018). In schools, this might mean establishing policies and procedures that promote inclusivity, respect, and equality for all students and staff. As Sara Martinez modeled at the beginning of this introduction, clear expectations and strong management are essential elements to creating a cohesive school culture (Michael, 2018).

- **U—Understanding:** To create a culture of belonging, it's important to understand and value the diverse backgrounds, experiences, and perspectives of everyone in the school community (Coetzee, Pryce-Jones, Grant, & Tindle, 2022). This might involve educating staff and students about different cultures and identities, and encouraging dialogue and empathy. As Sara's leadership story demonstrates, it's essential to seek understanding to solve problems and look for solutions within the school context (Michael, 2018).

- **I—Integrity:** Building a culture of belonging requires honesty, transparency, and accountability. Schools should be willing to acknowledge and address issues of bias, discrimination, and exclusion, and take steps to address them (Coetzee et al., 2022). Sara's story exemplifies the power of saying what you mean, choosing bravery over comfort, and adhering to one's values regardless of who is watching (Michael, 2018).

- **L—Listening:** Just as a builder must listen to the needs and preferences of their clients, schools must listen to the voices of their students and staff (Sullivan, 2018). Creating opportunities for feedback and input can help ensure that everyone feels heard and valued. Sara committed herself to walking the halls of her school and spent countless hours engaged in listening to staff and students to develop a better understanding of their circumstances. Through listening, we can truly learn to *hear* one another (Michael, 2018).

- **D—Dependability:** To build a culture of belonging, it's essential to be consistent and reliable in efforts to promote inclusion and equity (Sullivan, 2018). This might mean investing in ongoing training and support for staff or developing systems to monitor and evaluate progress toward these goals. Sara demonstrated committed focus on inclusion, pouring love into her school and managing through consistent practices, which yielded positive results academically and socially at her school (Michael, 2018).

Readers can connect each chapter's content to tangible actions that promote these essential elements of an inclusive educational environment. By focusing on these elements, schools can lay the groundwork for a culture of belonging and inclusion. Like a well-built home, a school community that prioritizes these values will be strong, resilient, and welcoming to all.

This book focuses on building strong and healthy relationships with others. By setting clear boundaries, seeking to understand others, acting with integrity, listening actively, and being dependable, you can establish trust and connection with those around you. It is an essential resource for anyone committed to fostering a sense of belonging in their school community. Through practical advice and real-world examples, this book offers a blueprint for building a positive school culture from the ground up. Let's work together to create a better future for our students and communities.

CHAPTER 1

THE FOUNDATION: BUILDING A CULTURE OF BELONGING

To be yourself in a world that is constantly trying to make you something else is the greatest accomplishment.

—Ralph Waldo Emerson

The crisp Midwestern air held a promise of new beginnings as Lucy stepped into the halls of Wheaton Elementary, the school that would become her new work "home." Moving from a small town on the West Coast to this sprawling landscape was not a journey she had anticipated. Leaving behind her roots, her students, and the coastal town that had always been home was difficult. She took a deep breath as she stood at the door of her new classroom, swimming in the uncertainty that lay before her.

The challenges were immediate. Memorizing new names and faces seemed like a daunting inevitability, but Lucy was surprised by the skeptical looks of parents, the cool glances from colleagues, and the blatant disrespect of her new students, who seemed to think, "How long will this one last?" From the moment the bell rang, it was chaos. Throughout the day, students raced around the classroom, jostling each other, some refusing to start their work. Others walked right out the door whenever they felt like it, pushing one another. Immediately, Lucy felt out of her depth, missing the simplicity of her previous life, where the rhythm was familiar and predictable. How would she teach them? Day after day, her initial excitement quickly melted into discouragement.

Each evening, she returned home depleted, questioning her ability to make a difference in her new role. Her stress spilled over into her personal life. Although she was exhausted from the day, she struggled to sleep. She stopped taking calls from her family, since she felt she had no time, drowning in marking and prep for the new curriculum. Every morning, she awoke with a sense of dread.

One day, as Lucy emerged from her classroom with tears brimming in her eyes, she felt a gentle hand on her shoulder. Turning, she saw Tanya, a fellow teacher who taught down the hall. Without a word, Tanya enveloped Lucy in a warm embrace, offering silent solidarity. Tanya invited Lucy out for coffee, sensing her need for support. As Lucy expressed her frustrations and challenges, Tanya listened. It was a turning point.

For the first time in weeks, Lucy did not feel alone. Tanya reminded her that taking care of herself was vital if she was going to make it through the year. Tanya invited Lucy to join the weekly Friday teacher get-together at the local coffee shop. She told her that taking charge is an essential part of creating boundaries with a new class. "They'll respect you more for it," she said.

After their meeting, something shifted in Lucy. She leaned into her new friendships, finding support and solutions within her community. She began to appreciate the beauty of her surroundings and the opportunity for growth. Quality time with her loved ones became a priority again; calls from her family on Sunday evenings filled her with gratitude before each school week.

As weeks turned into months, Lucy's resilience grew, fueled by the support of her newfound friendships and the strength of her own determination. She began to see glimpses of progress in her students, small victories that affirmed her belief in the transformative power of education. That year, Lucy discovered not only her capacity for resilience but also a newfound sense of purpose and belonging.

Lucy's experience serves as an example for constructing a sense of belonging. Initially met with chaos and uncertainty, she gradually found herself through community support and self-nurturing practices. Each connection and moment of resilience became a foundational pillar, anchoring her in her new environment. Tanya's friendship and support were an important cornerstone, providing guidance in times of struggle. Lucy's journey highlights the ongoing process of building belonging for yourself in the world of education, and emphasizes the importance of patience, perseverance, and adaptation.

Feeling like you belong in a community or group is essential for well-being, mental health, and academic success. As noted previously, Allen and colleagues (2018) find a correlation between students having a strong sense of belonging and higher grades, better mental health, and fewer risky behaviors.

While teachers and school leaders can build a foundation for a culture of belonging by fostering an inclusive classroom and school environment with strong boundaries, understanding, integrity, listening, and dependability, it is essential to consider your own ability to tune in and belong to *yourself* first (Michael, 2022). Actionable strategies for creating a culture of belonging—such as promoting student voice, providing opportunities for collaboration and peer feedback, and building strong connections with students—are essential to building a strong, positive school culture. And it all begins with self-leadership (Afsar & Umrani, 2020).

It's critical to understand that the journey toward creating a robust culture of belonging begins within us, as educators. Teachers, leaders, and paraprofessionals—the key shapers of educational environments—should first cultivate a sense of self-acceptance and belonging within themselves before they can successfully instill these values in school culture.

When educational leaders and educators experience a congruence between *who they wish to be* and *who they are*, they are not only more confident; they also are more capable of creating an environment that promotes authenticity and self-expression. This authenticity trickles down into the school culture, making students and other staff members feel valued and accepted (Michael, 2022). Leaders and educators who are authentic, know themselves, and are comfortable in their own skin can inspire others to achieve more than they thought possible. They are motivational figures who encourage authenticity, foster open communication, and promote individuality, all of which are key ingredients in cultivating a strong culture of belonging (Newkirk, 2019).

To create this culture, educators and paraprofessionals should first ensure that they are comfortable with who they are and that they belong to themselves. Once they fully accept themselves, they are better equipped to understand and appreciate the individual uniqueness of each student, encourage their growth, and foster an environment of acceptance and belonging (Brown, 2017). When teachers, leaders, and paraprofessionals foster self-acceptance and self-belonging, they set the stage for an inclusive and accepting school culture. In this way, the act of looking inward not only enhances one's self-concept and authenticity but also has the power to transform the overall culture of educational environments, creating places where everyone truly feels they belong (Newkirk, 2019).

When thinking of Sara's story at the beginning of this book, it's easy to see her ability to be authentic and confident. Leaders and educators like Sara operate from a place of self-awareness and emotional intelligence—characteristics that allow them to understand their own emotions and how they affect those around them (Brown, 2017). This empathetic approach helps them nurture inclusive environments where everyone feels that they are a valuable part of the team, even as they maintain their unique identity.

A Focus on Belonging to Yourself First

In the context of school culture, Brené Brown's (2017) work on belonging highlights the importance of authenticity and self-knowledge for educators and school leaders. Brown is a social worker, researcher, and author who has spent years studying vulnerability, shame, and belonging. Her work on belonging centers on the idea that true belonging requires authenticity and vulnerability. Brown (2017) asserts:

> True belonging is the spiritual practice of believing in and belonging to yourself so deeply that you can share your most authentic self with the world and find sacredness in both being a part of something and standing alone in the wilderness. True belonging doesn't require you to change who you are; it requires you to be who you are. (p. 37)

In her book *Braving the Wilderness*, Brown (2017) shares a personal story about her struggle with belonging as a child:

> I was raised in a culture that prized *fitting-in* over *belonging*. Fitting in is about assessing a situation and becoming who you need to be in order to be accepted. Belonging, on the other hand, doesn't require us to change who we are; it requires us to be who we are. (p. 38)

Rather than prioritizing fitting in and conforming to a particular standard or norm, true belonging requires individuals to embrace their authentic selves and have the confidence to share their unique perspectives and experiences with others. School leaders and educators who model this behavior can create a culture that encourages students to do the same, fostering a sense of belonging and connection within the school community (Allen et al., 2022).

By prioritizing self-knowledge and confidence, school leaders and educators can create a safe and supportive environment where students can develop a strong sense of self and feel empowered to share their authentic selves with others (Michael, 2022).

Five Strategies for Building Belonging as Educators and School Leaders

Belonging in education is crucial for leaders, educators, and paraprofessionals alike, fostering an environment where everyone feels valued, supported, and connected. Thinking back to Lucy's story, note that Lucy was able to employ several strategies related to self-care to foster belonging in herself (Kanold & Boogren, 2022). Among these strategies, which I write about in *From Burnt Out to Fired Up*, is the ability to reflect on current emotional and physiological states, reframe internal narratives related to current circumstances, refocus on a more compelling future of happiness and success, and reconnect with important people in one's life (Michael, 2022).

Drawing from the latest research and my own teaching experiences, I also identified five accessible strategies to reignite your passion and well-being: (1) reflect, (2) reframe, (3) refocus, (4) reconnect, and (5) reveal. Each of the following sections offers simple practices you can incorporate into your daily life to help you thrive and overcome the understandable effects of burnout (Michael, 2022). The following are some of the guiding principles that often help educators reignite their fire for teaching.

Reflect

Belonging starts with understanding and acknowledging one's emotions and needs. By encouraging educators to pause and reflect on their emotional states, you are promoting self-awareness and self-care, which are essential components of belonging (Carrington, 2023). When educators feel seen and heard, they're more likely to feel a sense of belonging within their school community (Michael, 2022).

Every day, and even several times a day, I encourage educators to pause to identify their emotional state through specific, actionable strategies.

- Identify your current emotions.
- Pinpoint your physical manifestations and stress points.
- Determine your immediate needs and communicate those with simple but honest language (Michael, 2022).

Reframe

Belonging involves creating a positive and supportive narrative for oneself and others. When educators reframe their challenges as opportunities for growth and learning, they foster a culture of resilience and optimism within their school community (Aguilar, 2018; Kanold & Boogren, 2022). By acknowledging support networks and effective self-care methods, educators realize they are not alone in their journey, further strengthening their sense of belonging (Michael, 2022). Consider exploring these questions in a journal to rethink the narratives you attribute to your current situation.

- What are the key challenges I've faced and overcome within the past year?
- Who are the individuals who provided me with support?
- What are the most effective self-care methods I employed throughout the past school year?
- What are my accomplishments and proudest moments in my educational role?
- What are the important lessons from the year?

Refocus

Belonging is about aligning one's goals and aspirations with their values and passions. When educators take the time to refocus on their dreams and goals, they reaffirm their sense of purpose and direction within the education system. The following offers a sequence of thoughtful reflections to help you refocus and incorporate goal setting into your foundational practices (Camp, 2017).

- What is one thing you would like to change about your current reality? Write down that goal.
- What is it about this goal that is important to you? How does it connect to the person you want to be or the life you want to live?
- How does this goal connect to your values?
- How might you feel when you have achieved the goal? What might a perfect day look like if you achieve the goal? Paint a picture by free writing this perfect day using all your senses to highlight this reality.
- What would it take for you to achieve this goal? Write down a list of actions you can take.
- Make a commitment to complete or perform one or more of these actions within a specific time frame.

Reconnect

Belonging thrives on meaningful connections and relationships (Carrington, 2023). By encouraging educators to cultivate strong communication skills and boundaries, you promote healthy interactions and connections within the school community. When educators feel connected to their colleagues, students, and support networks, they're more likely to experience a sense of belonging and fulfillment in their roles (Michael, 2022). The following are some ways you can encourage educators to stay connected in their personal and professional lives.

- **Online communities:** Engage in educational forums, social media groups, or platforms. Follow educational influencers and engage with relevant hashtags to stay up to date and participate in discussions.

- **Educational clubs and groups:** Initiate or participate in educational book clubs, study groups, or feedback exchange sessions to foster deep discussions and connections.

- **Local and virtual events:** Attend educational conferences, whether in person or virtually, and participate in local community workshops or gatherings to network and stay informed.

- **Personal connections:** Prioritize your personal and professional relationships, friendships, and familial connections through texting, phone calls, and emails (Michael, 2022).

Reveal

Many people mistakenly believe they aren't creative, forgetting that everyone inherently possesses creativity from birth (Geher, Betancourt, & Jewell, 2017). As adults, we often lose touch with our innate divergent thinking. To rekindle this creativity, it's essential to reintroduce playfulness and experimentation into our routines. In *From Burnt Out to Fired Up* (Michael, 2022), I encourage educators to explore novelty to access their creative identities. Engage in a new activity, like cooking, pottery, or painting, focusing not on the result, but on enjoying the creative journey itself. As educators, we can encourage students to do the same.

- **Engage in new learning:** Learn a new language, try a new recipe, explore a novel, try a new watercolor technique, or simply take a new route to work.

- **Get comfortable with discomfort:** Overcome your fear of failure, like podcaster Tim Ferriss (2009), and expose yourself to measured risk through comfort challenges that push you to explore relative discomfort to move beyond your fear of rejection and subsequent fear to be creative.

These strategies promote well-being and professional growth and can contribute to building a culture of belonging within educational settings. By prioritizing reflection, reframing challenges, refocusing on goals, reconnecting with others, and revealing creative identities, educators can create inclusive and supportive environments.

Belonging in Schools

When students feel like they truly belong in their classroom, amazing things can happen! It's like they have found their second home, a place where they are supported, valued, and accepted for who they are (Carrington, 2020).

> Serena had ambitions that always felt larger than what was currently offered in her little town. She dreamed of starting a business but felt isolated by her bold, audacious aspirations. Her high school guidance counselor introduced her to an online forum for young entrepreneurs. Inspired, Serena started a local group where she and other aspiring business-minded teens shared ideas, providing a supportive space for small-town big dreamers like her.

Students with a sense of belonging are more engaged in their learning, actively participating and achieving better academically. Friendships flourish, and a caring and inclusive community forms. They feel happier, less stressed, and more confident in expressing themselves. Belonging also helps students develop a strong sense of identity and resilience, encouraging them to persevere and bounce back from challenges. By fostering a culture of belonging in the classroom, you create a space where students thrive and find the support they need to shine their brightest (Carrington, 2020).

Sometimes, this can be as simple as offering students the opportunity to connect with their passions.

> In the heart of a small farming town, Mario's fascination wasn't with tractors, hunting, or camping—it was with computers. While his peers spent time making campfire memories, Mario was keen on coding. With support from his science teacher, Mario transformed a corner of a school storage room into a tech hub, inviting a few fellow tech friends to explore the digital world. Soon, after-school coding parties became a highlight for this tight-knit group.

Through the support of his science teacher, Mario was able to create a space where he and his peers could explore their interests and build a community around coding. This example underscores the importance of recognizing and nurturing individual interests and talents within the student body. By providing avenues for students to pursue their passions, educators not only cultivate a sense of belonging but also foster creativity, innovation, and personal growth. It's a reminder that every student has unique gifts waiting to be discovered and celebrated.

The following Classroom Toolbox and School Leadership Toolbox sections strive to equip educators and school leaders with the understanding and tools they need to foster a sense of positivity and belonging in their schools.

CLASSROOM TOOLBOX

> By focusing on the BUILD elements—boundaries, understanding, integrity, listening, and dependability—teachers can use these activities to foster positive relationships and a sense of belonging in their classroom. Note that elements do not need to be sequential, and some activities address more than one element.

Psychological Safety in the Classroom

⊘ Boundaries

Building safety can help create a culture of trust and psychological safety in the classroom. It is important to remember that psychological safety is "a belief that one will not be punished or humiliated for speaking up with ideas, questions, concerns or mistakes" (Zaidi, 2022, p. 38). This involves creating clear expectations and norms, providing feedback and support, and celebrating progress and achievements (Coyle, 2018). The following are some strategies for providing a psychologically safe classroom environment for students.

1. **Collaboratively establish expectations:** Engage students in a discussion to establish safety norms and expectations for the classroom. Encourage open dialogue, active participation, and mutual respect. Facilitate a brainstorming session in which students can share their thoughts and ideas about what makes them feel safe and supported in the learning environment.

2. **Create a visual representation:** Once you establish expectations, collaboratively create a visual representation of the safety norms. This can be in the form of a classroom poster, a set of classroom rules, or even a student-created charter. Students can create flyers using programs such as Canva for Education (https://canva.com/learn/how-to-use-canva-for-education), draw or gather visuals to represent each of the expectations, or take pictures of students demonstrating desired behaviors. Involve students in the design process, allowing them to express their creativity and ownership in shaping the visual representation.

3. **Reinforce and regularly review norms:** Consistently reinforce the established safety norms by integrating them into daily routines and activities. Regularly review expectations with students, discussing their

progress and addressing any concerns. Encourage students to hold each other accountable and remind them of the importance of maintaining a safe and inclusive classroom environment.

Remember, establishing safety norms is an ongoing process, and it's essential to be responsive to the evolving needs of your students.

The Fire-Starter Question

♡ Understanding

The fire-starter question can help generate momentum and engagement with others. This strategy involves asking a series of questions to help someone identify a topic or issue to explore further (Stanier, 2016). While this strategy has been used in business to create strong workplace cultures for employees, this approach is also helpful in a school setting. Build strong connections with students by greeting them at the door, making time for individual conversations, and displaying interest and understanding in their lives outside of school. For example, greet each student by name as they enter the classroom and schedule regular one-on-one check-ins with them. The following are some questions to start off the conversation.

- "What is something you're looking forward to today?"
- "Is there anything you would like to share or discuss with the class today?"
- "What is something interesting you can share that you learned or discovered outside of school?"
- "Who is someone in our classroom that you appreciate and why?"
- "How can we support each other in achieving our goals today?"
- "What's the funniest thing that happened to you recently?"
- "If you could travel anywhere in the world right now, where would you go?"
- "If you could have a superpower for a day, what would it be and how would you use it?"
- "What's your favorite song to sing along to when nobody's listening?"
- "If you could have a magical breakfast, what would it include?"
- "What's one thing that always makes you smile?"
- "What's your favorite thing about coming to school?"

- "What's one thing you've been proud of accomplishing recently?"
- "What's the best thing that has happened to you since we last saw each other?"

These lighthearted questions can help create a positive and joyful atmosphere in the morning, allowing students to share their imaginations, laughter, and unique perspectives.

Feelings Reflections

Understanding

Reflecting a student's feelings can help them feel validated and understood. This strategy involves acknowledging and labeling the student's emotions without judgment. It can help them feel heard and lead to productive conversations (Rolland, 2022). The following are a few ways to explore feelings and emotions with students.

- **Emotions charades:** Have students take turns acting out different emotions without using words while the rest of the class tries to guess the emotion they're portraying. This activity encourages students to use body language and facial expressions to convey feelings (Pons, Harris, & Doudin, 2002).
- **Feelings journal:** Provide each student with a small notebook or journal dedicated to expressing their feelings. Set aside a few minutes each day or week for students to write or draw about how they are feeling. Encourage them to be honest and reflective and emphasize that their feelings are valid.
- **Emotions circle:** Form a circle with students and take turns sharing an emotion they are currently experiencing. Encourage them to explain why they feel that way. This exercise helps students practice identifying and articulating their emotions while fostering a supportive and empathetic classroom environment.

Empowerment With Student Voice and Choice

Integrity

Promote student voice and choice by providing opportunities for students to share their opinions and ideas, and take ownership of their learning (Mitra, 2006). For example, implement regular class meetings in which students can share their ideas and opinions about classroom decisions, and create opportunities for student-led projects and presentations. A research study by Dana Mitra (2006) reveals that when students feel heard and valued in their educational environment, their sense of self-worth and belonging significantly improves. She explores how student voice (how students articulate their interests, needs, and perspectives in the educational environment) positively impacts their overall educational experience and self-concept as learners (Mitra, 2006). The study found that students who had the opportunity to express their opinions and make choices about their learning demonstrated greater engagement, higher academic achievement, and a stronger connection to their school community. The following are five ways you can integrate voice and choice within the classroom.

1. **Student-led discussions:** Provide opportunities for students to lead class discussions or share their thoughts and opinions on various topics. Encourage active participation and respectful listening to create a classroom culture where everyone's voice is valued. Offer to house an anonymous question or discussion prompt box in the classroom that allows students to generate topics the class can address during morning meetings.

2. **Choice in assignments:** Offer students choices in assignments or projects whenever possible. Allow them to select topics of interest or determine the format in which they showcase their learning. This fosters a sense of ownership and autonomy, promoting engagement and investment in their education.

3. **Collaborative decision making:** Involve students in decision-making processes that affect the classroom. Seek their input on rules, routines, or classroom activities, and encourage them to contribute ideas and suggestions. This empowers students, making them feel valued and invested in their learning environment.

4. **Peer feedback and reflection:** Incorporate peer feedback and reflection activities in which students can provide constructive input for their peers' work. This cultivates a supportive classroom community and promotes collaboration, empathy, and communication skills.

5. **Student-led initiatives:** Encourage students to take the lead in organizing events, projects, or initiatives within the classroom or school. This empowers them to take ownership of their learning environment and develop leadership skills. Empowering students to drive change and make a positive impact reinforces a sense of belonging and purpose.

By incorporating these strategies, you can create a classroom environment that values student voice and choice, fostering a sense of belonging, ownership, and empowerment among your students.

Active Listening

🔊 Listening

Active listening involves paying full attention to someone's words, showing interest and empathy, and avoiding distractions. This strategy helps build trust and understanding between and among adults and children (Rolland, 2022). Help students learn active listening skills by doing the following.

1. **Model active listening:** Demonstrate active listening skills by maintaining eye contact, nodding, and providing verbal cues to show that you are engaged and attentive when others speak. Use visuals and reminders to draw students' attention to active listening throughout the day.

2. **Practice taking turns:** Encourage students to take turns speaking and listening in conversations or group discussions. Teach them to wait patiently without interrupting and respond thoughtfully after the speaker has finished.

3. **Use listening activities:** Engage students in interactive listening activities such as listening to audio clips, following listening-based instructions, or playing listening games. Then have students engage in activities to demonstrate their comprehension or a follow-up task. These activities can help develop their focus, comprehension, and receptive abilities.

Morning Meetings

🛡 Dependability

Morning meetings are practical venues for sharing information and establishing classroom norms, as well as a powerful means of fostering a positive and inclusive school culture. They offer dedicated time for students and teachers to come together, building a sense of community and belonging. These gatherings create opportunities for deep social learning, allowing students to practice essential skills like active listening, respectful communication, and problem solving.

These meetings are typically held in classrooms or schoolwide, and can serve several purposes, including the following.

- **Building community:** Morning meetings can help create a sense of belonging and connection among students and teachers.

- **Sharing important information:** Teachers can use morning meetings to communicate announcements, upcoming events, and any changes to the schedule.

- **Fostering social-emotional learning (SEL):** Morning meetings can provide a space for students to practice important skills such as active listening, respectful communication, and problem solving.

Educator and author Monica Dunbar (2020) offers the following suggestions for running an effective morning meeting.

1. **Determine the purpose and agenda of the meeting:** Consider what topics you want to cover and what outcomes you hope to achieve.

2. **Set a consistent time and location:** Choose a time that works for everyone, such as the beginning of the school day, and a location that is accessible for all students.

3. **Establish routines:** Consider incorporating a consistent structure or routine for the meeting, such as a greeting, sharing time, and a closing activity.

4. **Engage students:** Encourage student participation and give them opportunities to lead and contribute to the meeting.

5. **Provide support:** Be mindful of students' needs and provide support when necessary, such as by using visuals or providing additional language support.

SCHOOL LEADERSHIP TOOLBOX

> By focusing on the BUILD elements—boundaries, understanding, integrity, listening, and dependability—school leaders can use these activities to foster a sense of belonging in their school.

Start With School Culture

⊘ Boundaries

Establishing schoolwide expectations helps create a sense of normalcy and routine for students and staff. This strategy involves reviewing and reteaching school expectations, routines, and procedures; creating a positive and respectful classroom environment; and setting clear boundaries and consequences for all (American Psychological Association, n.d.). It also means creating clear and consistent schoolwide expectations for behavior and conduct (Colvin & Sugai, 2018). The following are some steps for creating these expectations.

1. Develop a committee or task force to establish the expectations for behavior and conduct.
2. Involve teachers, students, parents, and administrators in the development process to ensure inclusivity and buy-in.
3. Clearly communicate the expectations to all stakeholders, including written policies and visual aids such as posters.
4. Consistently enforce the expectations to ensure accountability and reinforce positive behavior.
5. Regularly review and revise the expectations to ensure relevance and effectiveness.

For example, a committee of teachers, students, parents, and administrators can work together to establish a set of behavior expectations, such as *be respectful*, *be responsible*, and *be safe*. The committee then clearly communicates these expectations through posters in classrooms and hallways, as well as written policies shared with parents and students. Teachers consistently enforce the expectations in their classrooms, and administrators provide additional support and resources as needed. At the end of each school year, the committee reviews and revises the expectations based on feedback from stakeholders.

The Focus Challenge

♡ Understanding

The focus challenge is a simple strategy from Michael Bungay Stanier's (2016) book *The Coaching Habit*. This strategy can help prioritize goals and objectives for staff and colleagues within a school, as well as build understanding. It involves leaders and colleagues asking in a compassionate and curious manner what the essential root challenge is within a problem to help identify and understand the most important issue at hand and determine the best course of action during a strategic planning or faculty meeting (Stanier, 2016). This strategy is particularly effective when establishing new policies or procedures, or in anticipation of changes to workplace expectations and routines to build understanding with staff. Consider how the focus challenge works in the following scenarios.

- **Scenario 1:** During a one-on-one meeting, a teacher expresses frustration about classroom management issues. The principal decides to utilize the focus challenge strategy. The principal asks, "What specific behaviors are you noticing in your classroom?" After the teacher explains, the principal follows up with, "What do you think might be contributing to these behaviors?" Through this compassionate and curious inquiry, the principal helps the teacher pinpoint the underlying challenges, such as inconsistent routines or lack of student engagement. Together, they brainstorm strategies to address these issues effectively, fostering a collaborative problem-solving approach.

- **Scenario 2:** In a faculty meeting, a staff member raises concerns about student motivation and engagement. The principal, practicing the focus challenge strategy, encourages open discussion by asking, "What do you perceive as the primary obstacles to student motivation?" As teachers share various perspectives, the principal continues to probe with questions like, "What patterns or trends have you noticed in student behavior or attitudes?" By delving into the essential root challenge, the principal facilitates a deeper understanding of the issue among the staff. Together, they can then explore potential solutions and interventions to enhance student engagement and address the underlying issues effectively.

In both scenarios, the focus challenge strategy empowers the principal to support staff in identifying and understanding the core issues at hand. By approaching the conversation thoughtfully, the principal creates a supportive environment where collaboration and problem solving thrive.

The AWE Question

🔊 Listening

Another strategy Stanier (2016) developed discusses how the AWE question can help encourage self-reflection and insight in others. This strategy involves asking, "And what else?" after someone answers a question, prompting them to dig deeper and explore other possibilities or solutions (Stanier, 2016). You could ask this question during coaching sessions, one-on-one meetings, and monthly or weekly faculty meetings to prompt discussions and open dialogue. Additionally, you could utilize this strategy when implementing morning meetings. This strategy offers all stakeholders an opportunity to expand on their perceived experience as well as work toward being understood and heard. Consider how educators used the AWE question strategy in the following scenario.

> During a meeting with a concerned parent regarding their child's academic performance, the principal senses that the parent is holding back some concerns or questions. Wanting to ensure that the parent feels heard and understood, the principal decides to apply the AWE question. As the parent expresses their initial concerns about their child's grades and behavior, the principal listens empathetically and then asks, "And what else?" This gentle prompt encourages the parent to delve deeper into their thoughts and feelings, allowing them to express any additional concerns or perspectives they may have.
>
> On hearing the question, the parent pauses, realizing there are indeed other aspects of their child's academic experience they wish to discuss. They share further concerns about their child's social interactions at school and potential underlying reasons for their struggles. This additional information provides valuable insight for the principal, enabling them to address the parent's concerns more comprehensively.

By using the AWE question during the difficult parent conversation, the principal demonstrates a commitment to fostering open dialogue and understanding.

New Teacher and Student Onboarding

🛡 Dependability

There are several unique onboarding routines and traditions from top companies you could apply to building positive school culture through new teacher and student onboarding, which reinforce school norms, routines, and values. While the principal may be responsible for initiating these procedures, a diverse school-based committee could easily spearhead these efforts. The following are a few examples.

- **Welcome letters from senior leadership:** Google is known for sending personalized welcome letters to new hires from senior leadership, including the CEO (Bock, 2015). The letter outlines the company's mission, values, and culture, and welcomes the new employee to the team. Schools can adapt this approach to provide a similar introduction to the school's mission, values, and culture.

    - *For new teachers,* the principal could send personalized welcome letters highlighting the school's mission, vision, values, and culture. The letter could include a warm introduction from the principal, an overview of the school's educational philosophy, and information about key staff members and resources available for support.

    - *For new students,* the principal can send welcome letters to both the new student and their family, introducing them to the school community. The letter includes information about school policies, academic programs, extracurricular activities, and resources for academic and social support.

- **Buddy programs:** Many companies, including Facebook, have a buddy system in which new employees are paired with a more experienced colleague who can help them navigate the company culture and provide support (Sandberg, 2013). Schools can implement a similar program, pairing new students with a mentor or "buddy" who can help them adjust to the school environment.

    - *For new teachers,* the principal could assign each a mentor from the existing faculty who provides guidance and support during their transition. The mentor could assist with navigating school policies and procedures, understanding curriculum expectations, and integrating into the school community.

- *For new students,* the principal could establish a peer-mentoring program where experienced students volunteer to serve as buddies. These peer mentors can help new students acclimate to the school environment, show them around campus, introduce them to classmates, and provide support and friendship during their first few weeks at school.

- **Onboarding events:** LinkedIn hosts a two-day orientation program for new hires, which includes sessions on the company's culture, strategy, and products, as well as opportunities to meet with senior executives and network with other new employees (Hoffman, Casnocha, & Yeh, 2014). Schools can hold similar events to introduce new students and their families to the school community, including administrators, faculty, staff, and other families.

  - *For new teachers,* the principal could organize a comprehensive orientation program spanning multiple days and covering various aspects of school culture, curriculum, and professional development opportunities. The program could include sessions led by senior leadership, department heads, and experienced teachers, as well as networking opportunities with colleagues.

  - *For new students,* the principal could host orientation events for them and their families, providing tours of the school facilities, introductions to teachers and staff, and information sessions on academic programs, extracurricular activities, and support services available. These events could also include interactive activities and icebreakers to help new students connect with peers.

- **Culture videos:** Zappos, an online shoe and clothing retailer, is famous for its culture videos, which showcase the company's unique culture and values (Hsieh, 2010). Schools can create similar videos to showcase the school's culture and values, highlighting key aspects such as community, diversity, and inclusivity. Moreover, students could exercise their voice and choice by contributing to and even creating the videos themselves.

  - *For new teachers,* the principal could create a video welcome message, featuring interviews with current faculty and staff sharing their experiences and insights about the school culture, community, and values. This video could provide new teachers with a glimpse into daily life at the school and help them feel more connected to their colleagues.

- *For new students,* the principal could produce a series of videos showcasing different aspects of school life, such as academic programs, extracurricular activities, student organizations, and campus facilities. These videos could feature interviews with current students discussing their experiences and perspectives, giving new students a sense of what to expect and helping them feel more comfortable and excited about joining the school community.

- **Welcome gifts:** Airbnb gives new employees a welcome gift, such as a travel voucher or a set of luggage, to show appreciation and make them feel welcome (Gallagher, 2017). Schools can provide new students or teachers with a similar welcome gift, such as a branded backpack or school supplies, to help them feel more connected to and accepted within the school community.

  - *For new teachers,* the principal could prepare welcome packages that include school-branded merchandise, such as notebooks, pens, and a coffee mug, along with a personalized note expressing gratitude for their contributions to the school community.

  - *For new students,* the principal could provide welcome kits, containing school essentials such as a planner, school supplies, a school map, and a welcome letter from the principal. Additionally, the kit could include small tokens of appreciation, such as stickers or bookmarks, to make new students feel valued and welcomed.

Overall, incorporating onboarding routines and traditions can help create a more welcoming and supportive school culture, and help new students feel more connected and engaged with the school community.

Conclusion

In conclusion, the cultivation of a genuine sense of belonging in schools begins with the personal journey of educators and leaders toward self-acceptance and self-leadership. This journey forms the blueprint, guiding the construction process of a supportive and inclusive school culture. It's essential for these key shapers of educational environments to first embody the sense of belonging within themselves, thereby fostering an environment that promotes authenticity and individuality. The authenticity that springs from this self-leadership not only instills confidence but also cascades into the school culture, helping students and staff feel valued and accepted.

Furthermore, such leaders act as catalysts for open communication and inspire others to reach their potential. While strategies promoting student voice, collaboration, and strong connections form the bedrock of an inclusive and positive school culture, the journey toward a robust culture of belonging fundamentally begins within. As educators and leaders embody a sense of belonging within themselves, they provide a sturdy framework on which authenticity and individuality can develop within the school community.

To help you reflect on the learning in this chapter and set action items, complete the "Designing Your Blueprint: Laying the Foundation for Belonging" reproducible (page 38). You can find a completed example in figure 1.1.

REFLECTION POINTS	TAKE ACTION!
What are some things you do well to foster a positive classroom or school culture?	*In my kindergarten classroom, I always begin with a "soft start," in which the students spend the first ten minutes of their day with choice-based activities and parents are invited to stay. This gives me a chance to check in with students and parents.*
What do you wish to incorporate into your practice as an educator or leader that will create a better sense of community, a more welcoming approach, and a positive culture within classrooms and within the broader school environment? Use the BUILD acronym to incorporate all five elements of culture construction into your practice. Be specific!	**B (Boundaries):** *When establishing expectations, I like the idea of having students create their own visual representations of the expectations using technology.* **U (Understanding):** *During the morning "soft start," I use the fire-starter questions to guide relationship building with my students and families.* **I (Integrity):** *I dedicate some morning meetings to incorporating more student-led discussions and opportunities for students to share about themselves, using the "ask-it basket."* **L (Listening):** *During morning meetings in September, I encourage students to practice active listening not only within the whole group, but with each other, to encourage respectful dialogue for the year.* **D (Dependability):** *I co-create the routine for each morning meeting with my students and follow the routine to establish a consistent and predictable start to the day.*
How might you better serve your colleagues or the educators in your building so they can reach their highest potential? What is one strategy from this chapter you can commit to employing this week or this month? Be detailed in your response!	*I want to take a more active role in welcoming new staff to my school with a welcome note, introducing myself, and inviting them to join my team for a coffee visit after school hours their first week. Usually, I wait for the principal or office administrative staff to take on this role. Now, I want to take ownership of being a welcomer.*
Confidence and belonging often start from the inside. When it comes to self-leadership, what are some things you can continue doing to help ensure you feel wholehearted, valued, and significant in your role?	*I will reflect on some of the achievements I've made this year, journaling about them using some of the questions from the "Reframe" section in this chapter.*

Figure 1.1: Designing your blueprint—Laying the foundation for belonging.

Designing Your Blueprint: Laying the Foundation for Belonging

Take some time on your own, in a small group, or during a professional meeting or development opportunity to lay the foundation for creating a positive school and classroom culture.

REFLECTION POINTS	TAKE ACTION!
What are some things you do well to foster a positive classroom or school culture?	
What do you wish to incorporate into your practice as an educator or leader that will create a better sense of community, a more welcoming approach, and a positive culture within classrooms and within the broader school environment? Use the BUILD acronym to incorporate all five elements of culture construction into your practice. Be specific!	B (Boundaries): U (Understanding): I (Integrity): L (Listening): D (Dependability):
How might you better serve your colleagues or the educators in your building so they can reach their highest potential? What is one strategy from this chapter you can commit to employing this week or this month? Be detailed in your response!	
Confidence and belonging often start from the inside. When it comes to self-leadership, what are some things you can continue doing to help ensure you feel wholehearted, valued, and significant in your role?	

A Blueprint for Belonging © 2024 Solution Tree Press • SolutionTree.com
Visit **go.SolutionTree.com/SEL** to download this free reproducible.

CHAPTER 2

A POSITIVE SCHOOL CULTURE: FOSTERING GENEROSITY, KINDNESS, AND EMPATHY

A single act of kindness throws out roots in all directions, and the roots spring up and make new trees.

—Amelia Earhart

Paula King returned to our school after her spring break trip to Uganda with stories that captivated us all. A learning intervention educator at View Royal School, where I teach, Paula had visited a small orphanage turned school with about 150 students facing hardships beyond anything we could imagine. But despite their struggles, they found ways to be happy every day, like playing soccer with the soccer balls Paula had brought with her.

As I relayed Paula's stories to my own two children, also students at View Royal School, I could see the wheels turning in their heads. My eight-year-old daughter, Makena, always creative and artistic, said, "Mom, we have to do something to help those kids. We can't just sit here and do nothing."

My six-year-old son, Tyson, who loved baking, chimed in, "I can make cupcakes with little soccer balls on top. We can sell them and donate the money to the orphanage."

Excitement filled the air as they both began planning for the project. Makena spent the weekend making hundreds of earrings out of polymer clay, each pair unique and beautiful. She named the project Happy Ears for Happy Hearts and was determined to sell as many as possible. Tyson, with my help, spent hours in the kitchen perfecting his recipe for cupcakes with soccer ball decorations. The earrings and cupcakes were a hit with our family and friends, but Makena and Tyson were determined to do more. Together, they decided to sell their creations at local fairs and swap meets, and even at our school.

As Makena and Tyson worked tirelessly to make their project a success, I watched as they became more and more passionate about their cause. They researched the orphanage and shared their knowledge with others, sparking conversations about the importance of giving back to those in need. The impact of Makena and Tyson's project was immediate and far reaching. The sense of collective generosity and kindness that came from this project was palpable, and it brought people together in a way that was truly remarkable. It was clear that this had become more than just a fundraising effort—it had become a movement for good in our school community. This shared project of generosity created a sense of belonging that was felt by all, and it was a powerful reminder of the importance of coming together to support those in need.

Makena's and Tyson's two-week fundraising efforts raised over $500 for an orphanage in Uganda, enabling supplies, such as food and medicine, and improvements like a new tin roof for the leaky schoolhouse. Their commitment extended beyond fundraising, as they maintained connections with the orphanage through letters, pictures, and how-to videos for Makena's earrings. These videos inspired the children and adults at the orphanage to start their own sustainable businesses. Through their initiative, they became part of a larger community built on kindness, compassion, and giving. Makena's and Tyson's project, Happy Ears for Happy Hearts, not only demonstrated their compassion and initiative but also inspired a sense of collective generosity and kindness within their community.

In building a culture of belonging, fostering generosity is an essential pillar. Schools can lay the groundwork by offering opportunities for students to give back to their communities in the same way a builder lays the groundwork for a stable foundation. By participating in service projects or volunteering initiatives, students can contribute positively to society and develop empathy and a sense of social responsibility. To achieve this, many schools implement meaningful and impactful initiatives that address local needs and inspire collaboration, empathy, and positive change.

Generosity becomes a foundational building block for belonging. Research by Martin Binder and Andreas Freytag (2013) shows that people who give and volunteer are more likely to report higher levels of happiness, life satisfaction, and a sense of purpose. Encouraging generosity in the school environment can include creating opportunities for students to give back to their communities, establishing mentorship programs, and promoting a culture of gratitude and shared purpose, as we explore further in the chapter.

Teachers and school leaders can model generosity by recognizing and appreciating the contributions of their staff, students, and families, as well as offering their own time, expertise, and resources. As each act of generosity is added to the framework, the culture of belonging within the school grows stronger, creating a supportive and inclusive environment where all members feel valued, appreciated, and connected.

In *Cultivating Kindness: An Educator's Guide*, John-Tyler Binfet (2022) writes that kindness and positive relationships between students, teachers, and school leaders also have a significant impact on building a culture of belonging. Acts of kindness increase well-being, reduce stress, and create positive emotional experiences (Binfet, 2022). Simple yet impactful strategies for building kindness into the school environment include encouraging random acts of kindness (like opening doors for others; leaving kind, anonymous notes for others in their lockers; offering to help someone carry packages; or smiling at people as you pass them), modeling kind behavior, and teaching empathy and compassion. Teachers can focus on building positive relationships with students by practicing active listening, providing positive feedback, and promoting inclusion and acceptance (Binfet, 2022).

A positive school culture is essential for creating a culture of belonging (Coetzee et al., 2022). It promotes well-being, fosters student engagement, and encourages academic achievement. According to Jimmy Casas (2017), author of *Culturize*, educators and school leaders need to foster positivity through championing every student, maintaining high expectations of all stakeholders, contributing a positive outlook, and believing that every student can be a part of the richness of a school.

This chapter explores the research and strategies for fostering positivity, including promoting optimism, celebrating successes and achievements, and providing opportunities for students to develop their strengths and passions (Casas, 2017). Specifically, it examines the science of kindness, giving styles, the recognition gap, the contagion of incivility, and the concept of belonging through proximity. Next, you will learn about belonging cues that help *you* develop rapport and relate them to the vulnerability cycle. Finally, this chapter offers specific approaches to maximizing generosity within the classroom and school through actionable, research-based approaches.

Kindness as a Priority

Some might view kindness as a soft skill that is not crucial to organizational success. However, many successful educational organizations and companies across industries have prioritized kindness and empathy as part of their organizational culture (Binfet, Gadermann, & Schonert-Reichl, 2016). By fostering a positive work environment that promotes collaboration, empathy, and respect for all stakeholders, these organizations have achieved high levels of student and employee engagement and satisfaction, leading to improved educational and financial outcomes.

One exemplary model of corporate philanthropy is Salesforce's 1-1-1 model, which encapsulates the ethos of giving back to the community. Salesforce's approach designates 1 percent of the company's equity, product, and employee time to community engagement and philanthropy (Westwood, 2023). This initiative has led to substantial contributions, with more than $676 million in grants and 8.5 million volunteer hours, positively impacting 56,000 nonprofits and educational organizations (Westwood, 2023). Such a model can inspire educational settings to foster a culture of generosity and community service. Following are some specific ways this corporate approach could inspire change in schools.

- **Equity in action days:** Dedicate specific days throughout the school year when students, teachers, and staff can participate in community service or charity work, dedicating 1 percent of the school year to philanthropy.

- **Teaching tech for a good cause:** Facilitate a program in which students donate their time to teach technology skills to the community, which reflects service-based donations.

Zappos is another company that prioritizes kindness. In his book *Delivering Happiness*, Zappos CEO Tony Hsieh (2010) discusses the company's culture of happiness, which is based on the principle of delivering happiness to customers and employees alike. This culture emphasizes kindness, empathy, and collaboration, and has led to high levels of employee engagement and customer loyalty (Cancialosi, 2017). These examples can inspire school communities to focus on more explicit dedication to fostering positive culture.

- **Happiness committees:** Form committees or clubs that focus on creating joyful experiences for students and staff, such as surprise appreciation events or themed school days.

- **Empathy workshops:** Create regularly scheduled workshops for students and educators to practice and develop empathy, active listening, and conflict resolution skills, some of which I explore later in the book.

Patagonia is a company that prioritizes generosity. In an article for the *New Yorker*, Nick Paumgarten (2016) describes the company's values-based culture, which prioritizes kindness and respect for all stakeholders, including employees, customers, and the environment. Patagonia encourages employees to participate in volunteer activities and prioritize work-life balance, which has led to high levels of employee satisfaction and retention. In 2022, Yvon Chouinard, the company's founder, pledged to donate all profits to environmental causes. Patagonia's dedication to generosity and environmental stewardship can be an inspiration for schools. Here are some ideas to weave this spirit of generous environmentalism into your school.

- **Environmental clubs:** Support or create student-led environmental clubs that engage in local and global initiatives, reflecting Patagonia's commitment to the planet.
- **Volunteer time off:** Provide students with opportunities to take time from regular classes or after school to volunteer, similar to Patagonia's support for employee volunteering.

Finally, Google has highlighted kindness by creating a positive work environment that promotes collaboration and well-being. In his book *Work Rules!*, former Google executive Laszlo Bock (2015) describes how the company encourages employees to take breaks, participate in team-building activities, and prioritize their mental and physical well-being. These initiatives have led to high levels of employee engagement and satisfaction. Here are a few changes your school might wish to make, inspired by this corporate initiative.

- **Innovation time off:** Allow students to spend a portion of their time on passion projects, akin to Google's 20 percent time, which gives employees time to work on projects they're passionate about.
- **Team-building retreats:** Organize retreats or field trips that focus on team building and interpersonal skills, supporting the kind of collaboration Google encourages.

Overall, these examples demonstrate that kindness and empathy are not just "nice to have" qualities; they are essential to creating a positive work environment that fosters collaboration, engagement, and business success. Leaders who prioritize kindness can create a culture of respect and empathy that leads to improved employee satisfaction, retention, and customer loyalty. The examples of companies prioritizing true kindness across industries demonstrate the importance of fostering a positive work environment that values empathy, collaboration, and respect for all stakeholders. However, the impact of kindness is not limited to business organizations. In fact, the principles of kindness and empathy are also essential for effective leadership and education (Enkel & Bader, 2016).

Effective leadership is about not just achieving results, but also building relationships and creating a culture of trust, respect, and empathy. Leaders who prioritize kindness and empathy are more likely to inspire and motivate team members, leading to improved engagement, satisfaction, and productivity (Enkel & Bader, 2016). Moreover, leaders who model kindness and empathy can create a ripple effect throughout their organization, encouraging others to behave in a similar manner.

Education is about not just imparting knowledge but also fostering social and emotional development. In fact, research conducted by Joseph Durlak, Roger Weissberg, Allison Dymnicki, Rebecca Taylor, and Kriston Schellinger (2011) indicates that social-emotional learning is essential for student success, both academically and personally. SEL focuses on skills such as self-awareness, empathy, communication, and conflict resolution, which are crucial for developing positive relationships, managing emotions, and making responsible decisions (Durlack et al., 2011). In the following scenario, Oscar's teacher demonstrates kindness to him, which significantly impacts his life and his sense of belonging.

> Oscar grew up in a small rural town. As a young child, he was fascinated with the stars and how the universe was a mystery to be explored. His dreams of exploring astronomy seemed out of reach until his science teacher lent him a telescope. This small act of intentional kindness made a significant difference. Sharing this passion, Oscar and his teacher started a monthly stargazing club at school. With minimal light pollution, the school's field became the perfect spot for the community to come together and explore the night sky.

Looking to other industries for best practice is essential for improving leadership in education. By examining successful organizations that prioritize kindness and empathy, educators can learn from their strategies and apply them to their own contexts. This process of cross-industry learning can lead to improved outcomes and greater innovation (Enkel & Bader, 2016). For example, incorporating generosity into educational settings can be achieved by transforming the classroom environment to be more student-centric and collaborative. Seating arrangements should encourage interaction; student-centered spaces can cater to various learning activities, and student work should be displayed to build ownership and pride.

Personalizing spaces with elements that reflect students' identities and shared classroom responsibilities fosters a sense of belonging. Welcoming colors and comfortable furniture create a positive atmosphere, while dedicated areas for collaboration and clear norms reinforce community values. Comfortable, inclusive seating options and accessible resources promote physical comfort and self-directed learning, thus emulating corporate initiatives to promote generosity and community engagement within the educational context. By creating a positive environment that fosters collaboration, engagement, and respect for all stakeholders, leaders can inspire and motivate their teams (Grant, 2013).

In schools, the kindness and generosity you foster can transform students' lives, just as corporate cultures nurture the talents and well-being of their employees. Take the story of Emily, for example. In her small town, where opportunities to pursue her passion for dance were scarce, she found an unexpected avenue to showcase her talent.

> Emily's small town had few opportunities for her passion: dance. Without a local studio, she felt her dreams were impossible to achieve, although she spent every waking moment dancing and creating choreography alongside her favorite social media stars. One day, her literature teacher—who was organizing a school play and knew about Emily's passion for dance—suggested Emily choreograph a dance for one of the numbers. The performance was a hit, leading to regular dance workshops led by Emily for her peers.

Connecting students with their passions can have a tremendous impact on their lives. Educators like Emily's teacher demonstrate a generous approach, propelling students on a trajectory that reflects the truest version of themselves. Their selfless investment in student passions underscores the profound impact of giving on individual and collective growth—a testament to the transformative power of kindness in education.

Giving Styles

Drawing inspiration from the corporate world's successful models of kindness and generosity, educators can look to interpersonal interaction styles to further understand and foster a culture of giving within schools. In his book *Give and Take*, organizational psychologist Adam Grant (2013) explores the different styles of interpersonal interaction that individuals can exhibit. Grant's (2013) insightful categorizing of *givers*, *takers*, and *matchers* offers a framework that schools can mirror to nurture a supportive and compassionate community.

- **Givers** prioritize helping others and contributing to their success, often without expecting anything in return. Givers in schools, such as teachers who stay after hours to help students or students who volunteer their time to tutor peers, foster an atmosphere of support and selflessness. Recognizing and celebrating such behaviors can encourage others to act similarly, creating a domino effect of generosity.

- **Takers**, on the other hand, focus on maximizing their own outcomes, sometimes at the expense of others. Takers who look to get more than they give can sometimes challenge school cultures. However, by acknowledging this style, educators can work on strategies to encourage more reciprocal or giving behaviors, such as implementing systems that reward collaborative success over individual achievement.

- **Matchers** strive to maintain a balance between giving and taking, seeking to trade favors and maintain a sense of fairness. Matchers operate on the principle of fairness, giving as much as they receive. In schools, matchers can help maintain balance, ensuring that giving is recognized and reciprocated. This can be harnessed by promoting peer-recognition programs where students and teachers celebrate each other's contributions.

According to Grant (2013), there is a difference between successful givers and unsuccessful givers. Successful givers are those who prioritize helping others while also looking out for their own interests. They can strike a balance between being generous and assertive, and as a result, they are able to achieve their own goals while also contributing to the success of others.

In contrast, unsuccessful givers are those who prioritize helping others to the detriment of their own interests. They may be too passive or selfless, putting the needs of others ahead of their own and neglecting their own goals and ambitions. As a result, they may not achieve the level of success they desire, despite their generous and helpful nature.

Grant (2013) suggests that the key difference between successful and unsuccessful givers is their ability to set boundaries and communicate their own needs and goals.

Successful givers can say "no" when necessary and prioritize their own interests when appropriate, without sacrificing their desire to help others. Unsuccessful givers, on the other hand, may struggle to set boundaries and assert themselves, and may end up burning out or failing to achieve their own goals.

By recognizing these styles, schools can tailor initiatives that encourage more giving behaviors, call out toxic behavior, and maintain a fair and supportive environment. Ultimately, understanding these styles can lead to a more empathetic, collaborative, and kind school culture.

The implications of these styles for the education environment are significant. In the classroom, students are also impacted by these styles. For example, givers are more likely to help others with their work and collaborate on group projects. Takers, by contrast, may be more likely to cheat or engage in behaviors that benefit themselves at the expense of others. Matchers may seek to maintain a sense of fairness and reciprocity, which can be beneficial in some situations but may also limit the potential for collaboration and collective achievement. It is essential for givers to develop strong boundaries and skills in assertiveness to maintain their sense of identity and achieve their own success.

Building a school culture that encourages giving behavior can have positive effects on both individual and collective outcomes, as demonstrated in Maya's story.

> In ninth grade, Maya experienced a major life shift. Her world changed when her family moved from a calm seaside town to a big, bustling city. Skyscrapers replaced trees, and quiet lanes gave way to busy streets. She missed the open spaces and familiar faces. One afternoon, her teacher noticed Maya drawing a park in her notebook and introduced her to a city-based nature club. The teacher's ability to see Maya's potential and interest in art, coupled with the effort to find and then connect her to this club, is an example of nontransactional kindness. The club's weekend trips to urban parks became Maya's refuge, reminding her that nature exists everywhere, even in concrete jungles.

A study by Joelle Ruthig, Tara Haynes, Robert Stupnisky, and Raymond Perry (2009) shows that students and educators who engage in prosocial behaviors, such as volunteering and helping others, have higher levels of well-being and academic achievement and overall job satisfaction. Additionally, creating a culture of generosity and collaboration can foster a sense of belonging and connection among students and teachers, which can improve engagement and motivation (Grant & Berry, 2011).

For example, a study by Kristin Layous, S. Katherine Nelson, Eva Oberle, Kimberly Schonert-Reichl, and Sonja Lyubomirsky (2012) finds that when teachers encourage students to engage in acts of kindness, such as writing thank-you notes to classmates or performing small favors, both givers and receivers report greater levels of happiness and well-being. When I think back to the way Tyson and Makena were able to make such a remarkable difference for the children in the Ugandan orphanage with the help of their school friends, it is obvious to me that this kind of community building is real, and the feeling of positivity is contagious!

By building a foundation of giving, schools can pave the way for a harmonious learning environment. Collaborative efforts, underpinned by a giving ethos, not only bolster academic success but also fortify the bonds of community and belonging within the school. While fostering a giving culture lays the foundation for a nurturing educational community, it is equally important to address and bridge the recognition gap, ensuring that every contribution receives the acknowledgment it deserves.

The Recognition Gap

The recognition gap between what employees need and what employers give is a growing concern in the modern workplace (Daimler, 2018). In his book, *Rewarding Performance: Guiding Principles; Custom Strategies*, Robert J. Greene (2019) asserts that recognition is a key driver of employee engagement and motivation, yet many organizations fail to provide the level of recognition that employees desire. A study by human resource management company Workhuman (2017) finds that employees who receive regular recognition are more likely to be engaged, have higher job satisfaction, and are more committed to their organization. Yet only 23 percent of employees report receiving recognition on a weekly basis, and 34 percent report that they have never received recognition from their manager.

In educational settings, the recognition gap can manifest in various ways that affect educators and their sense of value within the school community. For example:

- An educator consistently stays late to help students with their work, yet their extra efforts go unnoticed during staff meetings or performance reviews.
- An educator develops innovative teaching methods that significantly improve student engagement, but the school administration does

not acknowledge these achievements or share them as best practices with staff.

- An educator goes beyond the curriculum or the allocated financial allotments to support students' emotional and social well-being, but their work is not recognized as part of the school's success metrics because it is hard to measure.

- An educator leads extracurricular activities that contribute to the school's reputation and student development, yet these contributions are overlooked when discussing career advancement or incentives.

Addressing the recognition gap means ensuring that such contributions are formally acknowledged, celebrated, and factored into professional development and advancement opportunities, which can lead to higher job satisfaction and motivation among educators.

The recognition gap can have significant consequences for organizations, including decreased employee engagement, higher turnover rates, and reduced productivity. To bridge this gap, organizations need to prioritize recognition and make it a key part of their culture.

According to organizational culture expert Melissa Daimler (2018), organizations can close the recognition gap by taking a strategic approach to recognition that includes setting clear goals, involving employees in the process, and providing regular feedback. Daimler also recommends using technology to make recognition more efficient and effective. The following are actionable ideas that can decrease the recognition gap in schools.

Teachers recognizing paraprofessionals can utilize the following.

- **Personal thank-you notes:** Write a personalized thank-you note expressing gratitude for specific contributions, such as assistance with classroom management or support with a student's learning plan.

- **Public acknowledgment:** During a staff meeting or in a school newsletter, highlight the paraprofessional's achievements, detailing the positive impact of their work on students' progress.

- **Professional development opportunities:** Advocate for the paraprofessional's attendance at workshops or trainings, acknowledging their potential and the value they bring to the team.

- **Shared success stories:** Share success stories with the rest of the school community regarding the paraprofessional's input, such as their role in a student's improved academic performance.

- **Award nominations:** Nominate the paraprofessional for relevant awards or recognition programs, either within the school or at a district level, to celebrate their dedication and hard work.

Principals recognizing teachers and paraprofessionals can utilize the following.

- **Recognition programs:** Implement a monthly recognition program in which teachers and paraprofessionals are awarded for their exemplary service, innovation in teaching, or contributions to the school community.

- **Spotlight in school communications:** Use the school's communication platforms, like the website or social media, to spotlight teachers and paraprofessionals, describing how their efforts have positively impacted the school.

- **Professional growth plans:** Work with teachers and paraprofessionals to create personalized professional growth plans that include opportunities for advancement, further education, and leadership roles within the school.

- **Dedicated appreciation events:** Organize special events, such as a breakfast or luncheon, dedicated to celebrating the hard work and commitment of the staff.

- **Inclusive decision making:** Include teachers and paraprofessionals in key decision-making processes, acknowledging their insights and giving them a voice in shaping the direction of the school's educational programs.

The recognition gap between what employees need and what employers provide is a real concern in schools and organizations. Organizations need to prioritize recognition and make it a key part of their culture to improve employee engagement and productivity. While addressing the recognition gap is crucial for fostering a positive work environment, it is also essential to tackle the problem of incivility, which can undermine the very culture of respect and appreciation we strive to build.

The Contagion of Incivility in Schools

Being consistently kind boils down to a fundamental question: *Who do you want to be?* This thought-provoking question was proposed by Christine Porath, a professor at Georgetown University's McDonough School of Business, author of the 2016 book *Mastering Civility: A Manifesto for the Workplace*, and presenter of the 2018 TED Talk "Why Being Respectful to Your Coworkers Is Good for Business." Porath's research-driven insights shed light on the negative impacts of rudeness at work, and show how practicing respectful behavior can enhance job success and contribute to a company's profitability. Her findings are not just confined to corporate settings but also resonate in educational contexts.

Porath (2018) argues that instances of toxic behavior, such as rudeness, gossip, derogatory texts, mockery, belittling, and overall disrespect, can trigger judgment errors, diminish performance quality, and cause chronic stress that potentially leads to health issues and increased mortality rates. According to a survey Porath (2016) conducted, over half the employees impacted by incivility cut back their productivity, 80 percent reported increased stress, and more than 12 percent left their jobs. The negative effects of incivility within a company's culture reportedly cost one organization more than $12 million annually. When these findings are applied to schools, they suggest that antagonistic work environments could contribute to teachers quitting the profession and experiencing elevated stress, depression, anxiety, and loneliness. This highlights the critical role positive school culture plays in educators' overall well-being.

Additionally, Porath's (2016) research reveals that rudeness is contagious and often culminates in a toxic work culture. One relevant study by Trevor Foulk, Andrew Woolum, and Amir Erez (2016) likens the contagious nature of rudeness in the workplace to catching a cold, revealing how the exposure to rudeness can increase the likelihood of individuals perceiving rudeness in subsequent interactions, which highlights the contagious effect of incivility within the workplace. A study by Eva Torkelson, Kristoffer Holm, Martin Bäckström, and Elinor Schad (2016) discusses organizational factors contributing to the perpetration of workplace incivility and emphasizes the contagious nature of such behaviors. People are affected to the extent that it can permeate all areas of their lives, including how they operate at work, how they relate to others, and whether they are effective or not (Porath, 2018).

Porath's (2016, 2018) findings provide important insights into the construction of a sense of belonging, particularly in educational environments. Incivility in these environments can manifest in various ways, impacting teachers, paraprofessionals, and principals alike, such as the following.

- A teacher openly criticizes a colleague's teaching methods in front of students or other staff rather than providing constructive feedback in private.
- A teacher consistently interrupts or talks over a paraprofessional during planning meetings, disregarding their input.
- A paraprofessional spreads rumors about a teacher or another staff member, which can create a toxic atmosphere.
- A paraprofessional shows a lack of respect for a teacher's classroom rules or undermines the teacher in front of students.
- A principal neglects to acknowledge the contributions of teachers or paraprofessionals during staff meetings or school events.
- A principal shows favoritism toward certain staff members without regard to merit, contributing to a culture of unfairness and disrespect.
- A parent aggressively confronts a teacher or paraprofessional about their child's grades or behavior in front of others, rather than seeking a private and calm discussion.
- Parents engage in hostile communications, such as sending disrespectful emails or making demanding phone calls that question the competence of the school staff without basis.
- A teacher or paraprofessional speaks negatively and unprofessionally about a student in a public or school-based setting.
- During meetings or school events, a parent interrupts proceedings, makes disparaging remarks, or refuses to follow the established protocols, showing a lack of respect for the school's operational procedures.

Each of these instances can erode the foundation of community and belonging that is essential for a supportive educational environment. Addressing such behaviors is crucial for maintaining a respectful and collaborative workplace. When an environment is characterized by incivility and rudeness, it doesn't just affect the individuals involved in those interactions. Even those who merely witness these negative behaviors can experience decreased productivity, and these effects can spread throughout the entire culture of the school or workplace, making it a toxic environment.

A negative, toxic environment hinders the development of a strong sense of belonging. If students or educators are exposed to this kind of negativity, they're likely to feel less safe, less valued, and less connected to their environment. This, in turn, can diminish their engagement, motivation, and overall performance, thereby negatively affecting their sense of belonging (Allen et al., 2018).

In contrast, an environment characterized by kindness and civility promotes feelings of safety and respect, essential components for nurturing a sense of belonging. When individuals feel respected and valued, they're more likely to engage fully, perform better, and cultivate positive relationships with others. This fosters a stronger sense of belonging, creating a cycle of positivity that benefits everyone in the environment (Binfet, 2022).

Therefore, it's essential to intentionally cultivate a culture of respect and kindness in schools to foster a robust sense of belonging among students and educators alike. By actively discouraging incivility and promoting kindness, schools can create an environment where everyone feels valued and connected, reinforcing their sense of belonging and contributing to their overall well-being and success.

Belonging Through Proximity

The Allen Curve is a concept derived from a research study conducted by MIT professor Thomas J. Allen in the 1970s (Allen & Henn, 2007; Waber, Magnolfi, & Lindsay, 2014). The main idea behind the *Allen Curve* is that the frequency of interaction between individuals decreases significantly as the physical distance between them increases (Allen & Henn, 2007). Allen found that when people are physically located closer to each other, there's an increase in the frequency of communication, even if the communication medium could theoretically allow for long-distance interaction (Waber et al., 2014). In other words, physical proximity has a profound effect on the frequency and depth of communication (Carrington, 2020).

In the context of creating a sense of belonging in an organization or educational institution, physical proximity and face-to-face interactions strengthen bonds between individuals. Despite the advent of digital communication tools, nothing quite replaces the richness of communication that occurs when individuals are physically close. The spontaneous conversations, nonverbal cues, and organic interactions that occur in these settings can foster a stronger sense of belonging and community (Carrington, 2023). Loretta Baldassar, Mihaela Nedelcu, Laura Merla, and Raelene Wilding (2016) and Kevin Harris (2003) highlight the critical role of physical proximity and face-to-face interactions in creating a sense of belonging within communities, challenging the notion that digital communication alone can sustain relationships and underscoring the unique value of direct interactions in fostering community ties.

Classroom design plays a significant role in creating a sense of proximity and belonging among students (Rands & Gansemer-Topf, 2017). For example, arranging desks or seats in a classroom that encourages face-to-face interactions can improve communication, collaboration, and a sense of belonging among students (MacKenzie, 2018). Similarly, in a school or organizational setting, creating common areas where individuals can interact informally can strengthen interpersonal relationships and build a stronger community (Rands & Gansemer-Topf, 2017). The following are several strategies to build proximity and foster a sense of belonging through classroom design.

- **Welcoming environment:** Use warm and inviting colors, comfortable furniture, and engaging visuals and images to create a positive and welcoming atmosphere (MacKenzie, 2018). Consider incorporating plants, natural lighting, and other elements that promote a sense of calmness and well-being.

- **Seating arrangements:** Arrange desks or tables in a way that promotes interaction and collaboration (Rands & Gansemer-Topf, 2017). Consider flexible seating options, such as grouping desks together for small-group work or creating a circle for whole-class discussions.

- **Comfortable and inclusive seating:** Provide seating options that cater to different needs and preferences, such as adjustable chairs, cushions, or standing desks (MacKenzie, 2018). This ensures that students feel physically comfortable and accommodated.

- **Student-centered spaces:** Create designated areas within the classroom that cater to different learning activities and preferences (MacKenzie, 2018). This can include a cozy reading nook, a collaborative work area, or a quiet corner for individual reflection.

- **Dedicated collaboration spaces:** Designate areas in the classroom specifically for collaborative work, such as group tables or a brainstorming wall (MacKenzie, 2018). These spaces facilitate communication, cooperation, and a sense of shared purpose among students.

- **Personalized spaces:** Allow students to personalize their learning spaces, such as providing bulletin boards or designated areas for displaying personal items or work that reflects their identity, culture, or interests (MacKenzie, 2018). This helps students feel a sense of ownership and connection to the classroom (Rands & Gansemer-Topf, 2017).

- **Student work displays:** Showcase students' work prominently around the classroom (MacKenzie, 2018). This not only validates their efforts but also promotes a sense of pride and ownership. It also helps students see their progress and accomplishments, creating a supportive and inclusive atmosphere.

- **Student-centered resources:** Organize resources, materials, and learning tools in accessible and labeled areas within the classroom (MacKenzie, 2018). This empowers students to take ownership of their learning and fosters a sense of belonging.

- **Shared classroom responsibilities:** Involve students in the decision-making process regarding the classroom environment (Rands & Gansemer-Topf, 2017). Seek their input on furniture arrangement, decoration, and organization. This encourages a sense of ownership and promotes a collaborative classroom community.

- **Classroom norms and agreements:** Establish clear norms and agreements about respect, inclusivity, and collaboration (Zaidi, 2022). Display these norms prominently in the classroom to serve as a constant reminder of the classroom community's values.

By implementing these strategies, educators can create a classroom environment that promotes connection and interaction, fosters a sense of belonging, and enhances student engagement and collaboration. These strategies send a powerful message that every student is valued and has a place within the classroom community. As educators lay the foundation for a nurturing and inclusive classroom environment, it's essential to pivot toward nonverbal communication. Belonging cues serve as the critical framing that offer the signals that support the structural safety and acceptance you strive to establish in educational spaces.

Belonging Cues

Belonging cues are nonverbal signals that create safe connections and show individuals they are valued and accepted (Maimon, Howansky, & Sanchez, 2023). These cues can significantly influence rapport building and cohesion within a group, leading to stronger interpersonal relationships and collective identity (Maimon et al., 2023). Belonging cues include signals like eye contact, active listening, mirroring or mimicking, body language, and verbal affirmations. Mimicking and mirroring are subconscious behaviors in which individuals replicate each other's body language, speech patterns, or attitudes, fostering a sense of similarity and rapport. Mirroring can lead to feelings of connectedness and trust.

When I am teaching, especially as I start co-creating expectations at the beginning of the year with students, I often guide students' attention toward the art of rapport building or belonging cues. Rapport building involves the creation of mutual understanding and positive relationships between people (Kim & Baker, 2017). It often involves showing empathy, respect, and genuine interest in others. When rapport is strong, people feel heard and valued, and are more willing to contribute their ideas and collaborate effectively.

The following are some common belonging cues.

- **Eye contact** demonstrates attentiveness and interest in the person speaking (Kim & Baker, 2017).
- **Active listening** involves responding appropriately to what others are saying, showing you understand and value their input (Maimon et al., 2023).
- **Mirroring or mimicking** reflects the other person's gestures, expressions, or speech patterns, indicating a sense of alignment or understanding (Maimon et al., 2023).
- **Positive body language**, such as open postures and nonthreatening gestures, signals acceptance and approachability (Maimon et al., 2023).
- **Verbal affirmations**, using simple phrases like "I see," "Go on," or "That's a great point," can validate others' contributions and enhance their sense of belonging (Coyle, 2018; Maimon et al., 2023).

The Vulnerability Cycle

Think back to a time when you crossed the colleague-to-friendship threshold with someone at your school, when you befriended a parent, or when you made the transition from acquaintance to friend in your own personal life. Often, the combination of belonging cues and a certain amount of vulnerability is the perfect recipe for truly feeling *seen* by others.

In his groundbreaking book *The Culture Code*, Daniel Coyle (2018) discusses the vulnerability cycle, a key mechanism in developing relationships and fostering a sense of belonging, especially in schools. It consists of two main components: (1) signaling vulnerability and (2) detecting that vulnerability. First, someone signals vulnerability, such as a student admitting they're struggling with a subject. Then, another person detects and acknowledges this vulnerability, creating an opportunity for reciprocal vulnerability sharing. This cycle leads to the formation of norms around when and how to express vulnerability and the types of support expected in the relationship.

For example, a teacher consistently responding with support when a student shares struggles can cultivate a norm of trust and open communication. Ultimately, this process increases closeness between individuals, fostering deeper relationships and a stronger sense of belonging. Schools can leverage the vulnerability cycle by encouraging openness and teaching students and staff to respond empathetically to others' vulnerability signals.

Coyle's (2018) vulnerability cycle includes the following steps, as demonstrated through the following scenario.

1. **Signal:** Olivia is struggling with a mathematics problem in class. Instead of keeping silent, she signals her vulnerability by raising her hand and admitting that she doesn't understand the problem.

2. **Detection:** Her teacher, Mr. Sanchez, picks up on Olivia's signal. He recognizes her struggle and validates her vulnerability by thanking her for her question and emphasizing that it's OK to ask for help.

3. **Signal:** Mr. Sanchez shares a time when he had difficulty understanding a concept, effectively signaling his own vulnerability.

4. **Detection:** Olivia and the rest of the class detect Mr. Sanchez's signal of vulnerability. They perceive this shared experience not as a weakness but as a humanizing and relatable aspect of their teacher.

5. **Norms:** Through these reciprocal vulnerability signals and detections, norms start to form in the classroom. These norms validate that it's OK to not know everything and that asking for help is encouraged and respected. This can also create a more supportive and inclusive classroom atmosphere.

6. **Closeness increases:** The ultimate outcome of this process is an increase in closeness. Olivia feels more connected to Mr. Sanchez and her classmates because they have all navigated this vulnerability cycle together. The whole class may also feel more cohesive and supportive, promoting a stronger sense of belonging for all students.

The same concept can apply to collegial relationships among school staff. For instance, a new teacher, Ms. Lee, might signal vulnerability by asking a more experienced colleague, Mr. Davis, for advice on classroom management. Mr. Davis detects this signal and reciprocates by sharing his own experiences as a new teacher, creating a shared understanding, and setting norms for mutual support. Over time, this vulnerability cycle can lead to increased closeness and collaboration among the staff, fostering a supportive and inclusive workplace culture. By encouraging these vulnerability cycles, schools can foster environments where students and staff feel safe expressing their challenges and seeking help, ultimately enhancing the sense of belonging and community.

The following Classroom Toolbox and School Leadership Toolbox sections strive to equip educators and school leaders with the strategies and tools needed to foster a positive culture in their school through kindness, generosity, and empathy.

CLASSROOM TOOLBOX

> By focusing on the BUILD elements—boundaries, understanding, integrity, listening, and dependability—teachers can use these activities to encourage and promote kindness and generosity in their classroom.

Ten Activities for a Kinder Classroom

🤝 Integrity, 🛡 Dependability

Kindness, an integral component of a positive school environment, is not just an innate characteristic but a skill that can be taught, nurtured, and practiced. By adopting a wide array of activities, such as kindness weeks, mentorship programs, kindness journals, and cultural exchanges, schools can foster an environment of empathy, respect, and mutual support.

These ten activities provide a comprehensive guide to cultivating a culture of kindness within your school. On my website and blog (https://morganemichael.com), I have compiled a series of tested and true lessons, activities, and demonstrations related to fostering kindness in schools and classrooms.

1. **Organize a kindness week:** Dedicate a week to various kindness-related activities such as peer appreciation, discussions about kindness, and acts of service within the school.

2. **Create a kindness wall:** Reserve a space where students can post notes acknowledging their peers' acts of kindness. This public recognition can create a ripple effect of positivity.

3. **Launch a "kindness rocks" project:** Encourage students to paint rocks with positive messages or images. Then have them place the rocks around the school, turning the campus into a canvas of positivity.

4. **Inspire the use of kindness journals:** Encourage students to keep a journal where they document kind acts they've done, received, or observed. This can encourage them to actively seek out and perform acts of kindness.

5. **Invite guest speakers:** Local community leaders or motivational speakers can talk about their experiences with kindness, imparting a valuable perspective to students.

6. **Give kindness awards:** Reward students who consistently show kindness. The awards can be certificates, badges, or even a mention in the school newsletter.

7. **Start a kindness book club:** Dedicate a book club to reading and discussing books that center on kindness, empathy, and compassion. This can stimulate important conversations among students.

8. **Establish a compliments day:** Set aside a day encouraging students and staff to give genuine compliments to each other, thus fostering a culture of appreciation and positivity.

9. **Establish a mentorship program:** Create a program that pairs older students with younger ones. This can help instill a sense of responsibility in older students and create a supportive community for younger ones.

10. **Create a kindness tree:** Create a bulletin-board tree display in a central location in your school. Each time a student performs an act of kindness, they can add a leaf to the tree, creating a growing visual representation of kindness.

Service-Learning Projects

Integrity

Create opportunities for students to give back to their communities through service-learning projects, volunteering, and community outreach programs. For example, partner with local organizations to identify service opportunities, incorporate service-learning projects into the curriculum, and provide resources for students to plan and execute their own community service projects. The following is a list of service-related projects you might consider for your school.

- **Community clean-up events:** Organize regular community clean-up events where families and students come together to pick up litter and beautify public spaces. This not only improves the local environment but also fosters a sense of ownership and pride in the community.

- **Food drives for local food banks:** Collaborate with local food banks to organize food drives where students and families collect nonperishable food items to donate to those in need. This addresses food insecurity and teaches students the importance of helping others in their community.

- **Clothing donation drives:** Host clothing donation drives where families donate gently used clothing, shoes, and accessories for individuals and families in need. This helps provide essential items to those facing economic hardships while promoting sustainability through recycling and reusing.

- **Environmental conservation projects:** Initiate environmental conservation projects such as tree planting, habitat restoration, or waterway clean-up efforts. These projects benefit the local ecosystem and raise awareness about the importance of environmental stewardship among students and the community.

- **Fundraising for educational initiatives:** Organize fundraisers to support educational initiatives, such as providing school supplies, books, or scholarships for students in underserved communities. This helps bridge educational disparities and ensures all students have access to quality learning resources.

- **Support for elderly or homebound individuals in the community:** Organize activities to support elderly or homebound individuals in the community, such as delivering meals, running errands, or providing companionship. This fosters intergenerational connections and teaches students the value of empathy and compassion toward others.

Overall, by engaging in meaningful and impactful initiatives like these, students can make a positive difference in their communities while developing important life skills such as empathy, leadership, and teamwork.

Follow these how-to steps to build a service-learning project in your classroom.

1. Identify a need or problem in the community that students can help address. Research and select a community organization or charity that addresses the need or problem. Use an inquiry-based approach to research the issue and to promote student-centered Universal Design for Learning. *Inquiry-based learning* is an educational strategy in which students follow methods and practices like those of professional scientists to construct knowledge (Kaçar, Terzi, Arıkan, & Kırıkçı, 2021). *Universal Design for Learning* is a framework for designing educational environments that enable all learners to gain knowledge, skills, and enthusiasm for learning (Basham, Blackorby, & Marino, 2020).

2. Contact the organization to arrange for a service-learning project, such as volunteering or fundraising.

3. Plan and execute the project and reflect on the experience with students.

Five Strategies to Build Community Using Belonging Cues

 Integrity, Listening

Use the following five simple belonging cues to build cohesion in your classroom.

1. Create a Culture of Active Listening

Teach and model active listening skills. This encourages students to value others' contributions and fosters a sense of belonging.

1. **Introduce active listening:** Explain the concept of active listening and its importance in daily communication. You can use a short video or role play to illustrate good and poor listening skills. Then ask students to practice the skill.

2. **Implement the pair-and-share technique:** Have students pair up with a classmate. One student shares a story while the other practices active listening, demonstrating understanding by summarizing the speaker's points.

3. **Reinforce with feedback:** Establish an active listening feedback loop for students to anonymously critique each other's skills. Continually remind students of the importance of active listening and integrate exercises throughout your curriculum.

2. Encourage Eye Contact

Promote the practice of maintaining eye contact during conversations (acknowledge certain cultural considerations or neurodiversities for students who may find eye contact uncomfortable or disrespectful) and signaling attentiveness and respect (listening). To internalize these skills, engage in a role-play activity. Start by demonstrating proper eye contact and then have students pair up for a fun game or conversation in which they can practice this technique. As they do, offer feedback and emphasize the importance of maintaining eye contact during class presentations and discussions.

3. Normalize and Encourage Nonverbal Cues

Teach students about mirroring and its benefits in fostering connection. Encourage its natural use in interactions. For example, when someone touches their chin or nods their head in a subtle way, mirror their actions by resting your chin in your hand or nodding your head a few times too.

4. Offer Regular Affirmations

Make it a norm to offer verbal affirmations during discussions with students, such as the following.

- "I appreciate your contribution here; it really broadens my understanding."
- "I hadn't thought of it that way; thank you for your insight."
- "I'm so glad you brought this up; you're right."
- "This is so important. Great reminder!"
- "Your ideas always bring a fresh perspective. Keep it coming!"

This reinforces the idea that all contributions are valuable.

5. Promote Positive Body Language

Teach students about the effects of body language on communication. Encourage open and welcoming postures during interactions to foster a sense of acceptance and inclusion. It's not just about words; it's how you stand, your facial expressions, and the gestures you make. Consider videos or images to highlight examples.

After demonstrating positive body language, encourage students to practice through role play, discussions, or presentations. Offer feedback on their efforts, spotlighting both their strides and areas to refine. Remember, practicing positive body language consistently in daily interactions will make it second nature.

Generosity or Gratitude Journals

☑ Dependability

Journaling is an effective tool for self-reflection and personal growth. Teachers can encourage students to keep a generosity or gratitude journal to record their thoughts, feelings, and actions related to generosity and gratitude.

1. Provide students with a journal or notebook.
2. Introduce the related concepts of generosity and gratitude, discussing the relative importance of both as reflective concepts.
3. Ask students to reflect on their own experiences with generosity and gratitude, and then record their thoughts and feelings in the journal. Students might express their gratitude for something kind someone did for them, or they might want to describe something kind they did for someone else.

4. Encourage students to set goals for practicing generosity and record their progress in the journal.

5. Discuss students' experiences with generosity and gratitude and reflect on their personal growth.

Storytelling

♡ Understanding, 🔊 Listening

Storytelling is a powerful tool for teaching character traits such as generosity. Teachers can use grade level–appropriate literature or real-life stories to illustrate the importance and benefits of generosity. The following is a list of books that focus on themes of kindness and generosity.

Grades K–2:
- *Last Stop on Market Street* by Matt de la Peña
- *The Invisible Boy* by Trudy Ludwig
- *Have You Filled a Bucket Today? A Guide to Daily Happiness for Kids* by Carol McCloud

Grades 3–5:
- *The One and Only Ivan* by Katherine Applegate
- *Because of Winn-Dixie* by Kate DiCamillo
- *Charlotte's Web* by E. B. White

Grades 6–8:
- *Out of My Mind* by Sharon M. Draper
- *The Giver* by Lois Lowry
- *Wonder* by R. J. Palacio

Grades 9–12:
- *To Kill a Mockingbird* by Harper Lee
- *Pay It Forward* by Catherine Ryan Hyde
- *I Am Malala: The Girl Who Stood Up for Education and Was Shot by the Taliban* by Malala Yousafzai

Each of these books offers unique perspectives on kindness and generosity, providing engaging narratives that can inspire young readers to embrace and practice these values in their daily lives. Use the following steps to explore these books with your students.

1. Select a grade level–appropriate book or real-life story that illustrates generosity.
2. Depending on grade level, read the story to students or assign it for students to read and then discuss its message.
3. Encourage students to reflect on the story and its impact on them.
4. Ask students to identify examples of generosity in their own lives and share them with the class.
5. Discuss the benefits of generosity for both the giver and the receiver.

Compliment Circles

Integrity,   Dependability

Compliment circles are a positive and uplifting activity you can use in various settings, such as classrooms, workplaces, and team-building events. This activity involves gathering in a circle and taking turns offering sincere compliments to the person to each participant's right or left. Compliments should be specific, thoughtful, and genuine. Compliment circles promote positivity, kindness, and teamwork by creating a safe and supportive space where individuals can express appreciation for each other's strengths and contributions.

Here is how to implement compliment circles in your classroom.

1. Gather students into a circle, in a random order, facing each other.
2. Explain the purpose of the activity, which is to build positivity and boost morale by exchanging compliments. This is a good time to explain that a *compliment* is a kind and positive statement you say to someone to show your appreciation or admiration for them. When working with older students, share research with them that supports and reinforces the contagiousness of positivity, so they understand the value of this activity.
3. Instruct the first person to pay a compliment to the person on their right. The compliment should be specific and genuine.
4. The person receiving the compliment should simply say, "Thank you," and then give a compliment to the person on their right.
5. Continue the activity around the circle until everyone has had a chance to give and receive compliments.

6. Encourage participants to actively listen and appreciate the compliments given to them.

7. After the circle is complete, ask participants how the activity made them feel and whether they noticed any changes in the group's energy or morale.

Figure 2.1 shows three different types of compliments and an example of each.

Tier 3:
CHARACTER COMPLIMENTS

These compliments highlight a person's character traits, such as kindness, empathy, or work ethic. They can be the most meaningful and impactful type of compliment, but they may also be the hardest to give.

Example: "I just wanted to let you know how much I appreciate your hard work and dedication. You're such a reliable and dependable team member."

Tier 2:
ABILITY COMPLIMENTS

These compliments recognize a person's skills or abilities. They may require a bit more thought or effort to give, but they can be very meaningful.

Example: "You did an amazing job presenting that project! You're such a great public speaker."

Tier 1:
SURFACE OR APPEARANCE COMPLIMENTS

These compliments acknowledge a person's physical appearance or style. They are easy to give and generally low risk, but they may not be as meaningful as other types of compliments.

Example: "I really like your outfit today! Those colors look great on you."

Figure 2.1: Three types of compliments.

*Visit **go.SolutionTree.com/SEL** for a free reproducible version of this figure.*

Celebrating the Wins

🤝 Integrity, ✅ Dependability

Celebrate successes and achievements by recognizing and rewarding positive behaviors and academic accomplishments. For example, create a positive behavior rewards program in which students can earn rewards for positive behavior and academic achievement. Incorporate regular celebrations and recognition ceremonies into the school calendar, and highlight student achievements through schoolwide announcements and social media posts.

The following are some specific examples of how to celebrate the wins and meaningful moments with students.

- **"Kindness coins" reward system:** Develop a school currency system in which students earn kindness coins for acts of generosity and compassion. Students can redeem these coins for privileges such as extra recess time, a pass to be the class helper, or a special lunch with a teacher.
- **Achievement wall:** Dedicate a bulletin board or a section of the hallway as an achievement wall where teachers and students can post notes or pictures celebrating both small and significant accomplishments.
- **Monthly recognition assemblies:** Hold monthly assemblies recognizing students for academic achievements, improvements, or exemplary behavior. Awards can include certificates, medals, or even titles like Student of the Month.
- **Digital brag board:** Use the school's website or social media platforms to create a digital "brag board" where you can highlight students' successes, allowing the community to celebrate together.
- **Peer-nominated awards:** Encourage students to nominate their peers for special recognition in various categories, fostering a supportive environment where students learn to appreciate and celebrate each other.
- **Positive behavior postcards:** Send home postcards or certificates to inform parents of their child's positive behaviors or achievements, strengthening the school-community relationship.
- **Special experiences:** Partner with local businesses or organizations to provide unique rewards, such as a behind-the-scenes tour of a museum, a visit to a local fire station, or a storytelling session with a local author or elder.

See Challenges, Not Failure

♡ Understanding

Foster a growth mindset by encouraging students to embrace challenges as opportunities for learning and growth. This approach, based on Carol Dweck's (2016) research, suggests praising effort over innate ability and viewing mistakes as chances for growth. Dweck's research distinguishes between fixed mindsets (where people see their talents as innate and unchangeable) and growth mindsets (where people believe they can develop their abilities through hard work and dedication). This concept highlights the importance of effort and resilience in achieving success and fostering a love of learning. For example, incorporate lessons on growth mindset and resilience into the curriculum, provide opportunities for students to reflect on their own learning and progress, and encourage them to set and work toward achievable goals.

The following is a list of actionable, classroom-friendly activities that can develop a growth mindset in students.

- **Challenge journals:** Have students maintain a journal where they write about a new challenge they faced, how they approached it, what they learned, and how they might handle a similar situation in the future.

- **Effort praise:** When giving feedback, focus on the effort and strategies used rather than the outcome. Phrases like "I can see you worked really hard on this!" can be more encouraging than "You're so smart!"

- **Mistake of the week:** Share a "mistake of the week" in class, discussing what went wrong and how it became a valuable learning experience, demonstrating that even teachers learn from their mistakes.

- **Growth mindset posters:** Decorate the classroom with posters that have growth mindset quotes and questions like, "What did you learn today?" and "How did you keep going when things got tough?"

- **Reflective discussions:** After a test or project, facilitate a class discussion on what students found difficult and how they can improve, reinforcing that challenges are a part of the learning process.

- **Role model stories:** Share stories of famous individuals who have overcome failure and emphasize the persistence they showed on their paths to success.

- **Brain education:** Teach students about the plasticity of the brain and how it can grow and strengthen with practice and learning.

- **Peer teaching:** Encourage peer-to-peer teaching moments in which students can explain concepts to each other, helping reinforce their own understanding and learn from different perspectives.

Belonging Affirmations

♡ Understanding, ⛨ Dependability

Affirming students' sense of belonging can help build their confidence and motivation. This strategy involves communicating positive messages to students about their ability to succeed and belong in the school community. This can be done through positive feedback, recognizing individual strengths, and acknowledging the value that each student brings to the community (Dweck, 2016). The following are a few classroom-based activities any teacher can implement.

- **Strength spotting:** Regularly identify and verbally acknowledge each student's strengths in front of the class to highlight the diverse talents within your classroom. Encourage students to do the same for each other. I often do this casually in our morning meetings.

- **Belonging rituals:** Create classroom rituals that celebrate belonging, such as a morning welcome or a handshake that reflects the inclusive spirit of the classroom. Have students create these together as part of their classroom community-building practices. This activity offers students with neurodiversities an opportunity to practice typical approaches to greetings and routines.

- **Peer recognition:** Encourage students to recognize and affirm each other's strengths and contributions, which you can facilitate through peer-recognition activities or awards.

SCHOOL LEADERSHIP TOOLBOX

> By focusing on the BUILD elements—boundaries, understanding, integrity, listening, and dependability—school leaders can use these activities to encourage and promote kindness and generosity in their school.

Show Your Gratitude

🤝 Integrity, 🛡 Dependability

Gratitude can help cultivate a positive and supportive work environment among teachers and staff. For example, during staff meetings, consider allocating time for teachers to express gratitude toward their colleagues for specific support or collaboration, such as helping with lesson planning or classroom resources. Starting meetings with an opportunity for participants to share something they are grateful for before moving on to more challenging discussions sets a positive tone for the meeting. This practice can build a culture of appreciation and teamwork.

Don't forget to celebrate collective achievements, such as improved student test scores or a successful school event, by acknowledging everyone's contributions, from teachers to custodial staff, highlighting the importance of every role in the school's success. Finally, don't underestimate the power of recognizing personal milestones like birthdays, work anniversaries, or significant personal achievements, which conveys that staff members are valued beyond their professional roles.

The following are several ways you can incorporate gratitude into your school environment.

- **Peer-to-peer recognition:** Set up a peer-to-peer-recognition program in which staff can express gratitude and recognize their colleagues for their contributions. For example, colleagues can display their recognition for others on a dedicated bulletin board in the staff room, adding encouraging or specific comments about staff members using colorful sticky notes. You could also encourage staff to share "bravos" or special thank-yous over the morning announcements.

- **Team meetings and school events:** Incorporate gratitude into team meetings or schoolwide events by asking employees to share what they are grateful for. Expressing gratitude can go a long way in promoting a positive school culture. For example, you can begin every meeting by offering staff the opportunity to celebrate each other and recognize special contributions to improving the school culture.

- **School connections:** Positive relationships with colleagues can help foster a supportive work environment. For example, LinkedIn hosts weekly "InDays" when employees can participate in team-building activities and connect with colleagues across departments (McQueen, 2015). On this day, educators and school staff can engage in peer-mentoring sessions, collaborative project planning, or even casual coffee meet-ups aimed at building positive relationships and a supportive work environment during professional development days.

Adapting this initiative for schools on professional development days encourages open communication, strengthens professional bonds, and promotes a culture of mutual support and continuous learning within the school community. Staff could set time aside to meet with colleagues to discuss grade-level topics, curricular outcomes, or yearly plans, using the opportunity to connect, plan, and align themselves about how to move forward together. Additionally, individuals within certain districts or divisions could offer to host professional development sessions about an area of expertise or passion to create in-house peer mentoring opportunities.

Encourage Vulnerability

Integrity

Encouraging vulnerability can help foster empathy and connection. This strategy involves sharing personal stories and experiences, modeling vulnerability and openness, and providing a safe space for others to share (Coyle, 2018). The most effective way to promote vulnerability is to model it as a leader. Through vulnerable actions, educators and school leaders can build a supportive, dynamic, and empowered school community where vulnerability is seen as a strength that drives connection, innovation, and growth.

The following are five examples of ways you can model vulnerability as a leader.

1. **Share personal experiences and challenges:** Leaders can demonstrate vulnerability by sharing personal experiences, including challenges and failures. This helps to humanize them and shows that they are not immune to difficulties. A good example of this is when Howard Schultz (2011), the former CEO of Starbucks, openly shared his story of growing

up in poverty, which inspired many of his policies at Starbucks, including comprehensive health coverage and stock options for employees.

2. **Admit when you don't know something:** It's important for leaders and educators to admit when they don't have all the answers. This not only shows humility but also encourages a culture of learning and curiosity within the team. For example, former U.S. secretary of defense Robert M. Gates (2014) was known for his willingness to express doubt and uncertainty, which in turn encouraged open dialogue and exploration of alternative viewpoints among his staff.

3. **Solicit feedback and act on it:** Leaders demonstrate vulnerability by actively seeking feedback from their team and taking steps to act on it. This shows that they value the opinions of team members and are willing to make changes. Ed Catmull (2014), co-founder of Pixar, implemented a process called the Braintrust in which filmmakers could give and receive feedback on their work, fostering a culture of candor and continuous improvement.

4. **Show emotion:** Expressing emotion appropriately can also be a way to demonstrate vulnerability. This does not mean leaders should be overemotional, but rather not shy away from expressing genuine feelings in appropriate contexts (Coyle, 2018).

5. **Empower others:** Leaders can show vulnerability by empowering others, delegating tasks, and trusting their team members. This shows that they are not afraid to rely on others. Google's Project Oxygen, a research initiative to identify key leadership behaviors, found that successful Google managers empower their teams and do not micromanage, illustrating the effectiveness of this approach (Garvin, 2013).

In the context of education, these principles of vulnerability and empowerment can be transformative when applied by teachers and school principals. For example, a teacher who shares their journey of overcoming difficulties in learning a subject can inspire students facing similar struggles. Such personal stories can create a bond of trust and motivate students to persevere. When a principal doesn't have an immediate answer to a schoolwide problem, openly stating so can foster a collaborative problem-solving environment, encouraging staff to contribute ideas and solutions.

When teachers show genuine care or concern, such as expressing pride in a student's progress or acknowledging the class's disappointment over a canceled event, they are exhibiting the kind of emotional honesty that strengthens relationships.

Establish a Shared Purpose and Goals

⊘ Boundaries, ☑ Dependability

Creating shared goals can help build a sense of purpose and direction in schools. This strategy requires involving all members in the goal-setting process and ensuring that everyone is clear on the school's mission and vision (Michael, 2022). Similarly, clarifying purpose can help align individuals and teams with a shared mission and vision. This strategy involves articulating a clear and compelling purpose, involving individuals in goal setting and decision making, and reinforcing the impact and value of the work (Coyle, 2018).

To foster a shared sense of purpose in schools, consider the following strategies.

- **Collaborative mission crafting:** Engage the entire school community in creating the school's mission statement through workshops and discussions.
- **Inclusive goal setting:** Involve students, staff, and parents in setting and reviewing schoolwide goals, ensuring everyone has a role in the school's direction.
- **Purpose-driven initiatives:** Launch initiatives that embody the school's values, like community service, to make the mission tangible and relatable for all members.
- **Transparent communication:** Maintain open channels for updates on progress toward goals, keeping the school's mission at the forefront of discussions.
- **Celebrating impact:** Share success stories that highlight the school's mission in action, reinforcing the collective impact of the school's efforts.

Designing Personalized Professional Learning

♡ Understanding

Designing personalized professional learning can help meet the diverse needs and interests of educators. This strategy involves providing opportunities for voice and autonomy, identifying individual learning goals and preferences, and incorporating multiple modalities and formats (Aguilar, 2018). Designing personalized professional learning for educators effectively addresses their individual needs and fosters professional growth. The following are three best-practice formats and some accompanying guiding questions to achieve this goal.

- **Individual professional learning plans (ILPs):** Craft ILPs for teachers, allowing them to set specific professional development goals that align with their interests, classroom needs, and career aspirations.

- **Choice boards:** Offer a variety of professional learning topics and activities in a choice-board format, in which educators can choose from a visual grid of available options, enabling educators to select the ones that most resonate with their current professional focus.

- **Micro-credentialing:** Implement a micro-credentialing system, in which educators can pursue short, bite-sized professional learning modules on topics of their choice, allowing for flexibility and depth in areas of interest. This could be something generated by the district to focus on specific topics, such as inclusive learning, numeracy, literacy initiatives, or other topics that relate to relevant mission and values, or it could be facilitated by external sources that the district approves as relevant professional development.

Ask teachers these guiding questions when considering professional learning opportunities.

- What are your current professional learning interests, and how do they align with our school's objectives?

- How do you prefer to engage in professional learning—independently, in small groups, or in larger workshops?

- What kind of support and resources do you need to meet your individual professional learning goals?

By incorporating these formats and reflective questions, schools can create a robust and responsive professional development environment that caters to the unique needs of each educator.

Strategic Questioning

🚫 Boundaries,   🤝 Integrity

Asking educators strategic questions related to their personal visions, goals, and wishes for their career can help promote clarity and focus. It is important to know your own limitations within the context of kindness and generosity. This strategy involves helping someone prioritize their goals and commitments by considering and reflecting on the question, "What do I have to say 'no' to if I say 'yes' to this?" (Stanier, 2016). To effectively manage one's time and energy in the spirit of kindness and generosity, setting clear boundaries is crucial. The following are a few strategies that can help in establishing limitations and maintaining healthy boundaries.

- **Communicate clearly:** Convey your availability and limitations to colleagues and students. For example, set specific office hours when you are available for meetings and consultations.

- **Prioritize tasks:** Make a list of tasks and responsibilities, then prioritize them according to their importance and urgency. This helps in identifying what you can realistically commit to.

- **Practice saying "no":** Develop the ability to decline requests that do not align with your priorities or capacity. A polite but firm refusal can prevent overcommitment and burnout.

- **Delegate responsibilities:** Identify tasks that can be shared or delegated to others. This not only helps manage your workload but also empowers others by giving them opportunities to contribute and grow.

- **Self-reflect:** Regularly assess your commitments and consider Stanier's (2016) question, "What do I have to say 'no' to if I say 'yes' to this?" This reflection can help in making informed decisions that align with your goals and capacity.

By using these strategies, educators can ensure that their acts of kindness and generosity are sustainable and do not come at the expense of their well-being or professional responsibilities. The truth is, it won't always be easy to set clear boundaries, but with time and practice, it will feel more and more natural.

Conclusion

In conclusion, generosity, kindness, empathy, and positivity form the cornerstone of a culture of belonging in schools. Evidence suggests that these elements not only foster happiness and life satisfaction but also bolster academic performance and overall well-being (Aguilar, 2018; Binfet, 2022). Initiatives such as community service and mentorship programs serve as the bricks and mortar, solidifying bonds within the school community. Meanwhile, a culture of gratitude acts as the scaffolding, supporting individuals as they navigate challenges and celebrate successes. Moreover, encouraging positive relationships through active listening and inclusivity binds the diverse elements of the school community together, creating a cohesive and supportive environment.

Establishing a positive school culture through thoughtful environmental design, belonging cues, authentic recognition and feedback practices, and opportunities to express vulnerability can reinforce a sense of community and belonging. By integrating these elements, schools significantly enhance their learning environments, fostering a sense of generosity and belonging among students, staff, and the community.

To help you reflect on the learning in this chapter and set action items, complete the "Designing Your Blueprint: Using Kindness as a Building Block" reproducible.

Designing Your Blueprint: Using Kindness as a Building Block

Take some time on your own, in a small group, or during a professional meeting or development opportunity to integrate kindness as a tool to bolster positive and inclusive classroom and school spaces.

REFLECTION POINTS	TAKE ACTION!
Name three ways you consistently encourage and recognize those around you.	
How does understanding the three different types of compliments impact how you might interact with peers, students, parents, and staff?	
What are some onboarding practices for new staff, students, and teachers you might try after learning some of the creative ways other organizations onboard new employees? What can you learn by cross-pollinating practices across industries?	

A Blueprint for Belonging © 2024 Solution Tree Press • SolutionTree.com
Visit **go.SolutionTree.com/SEL** to download this free reproducible.

CHAPTER 3

BIAS EXPLORATION: DISMANTLING IMPLICIT BIAS IN SCHOOLS

Bias is much bigger than prejudice. Prejudice is just the tip of the iceberg, while bias is the entire iceberg.

—LINDA DARLING-HAMMOND

Maria stands in front of her new class, ready to present her project on local animals. She recently moved to the United States from Mexico with her mother, who is completing a master's degree in engineering. As Maria speaks, her accent drawing out the vowels, a hand shoots up. "Can you say that again? I love hearing how you talk; it's so cute!" the student says, smiling. The class chuckles, and Maria forces a smile. She wishes the floor would just swallow her whole. The pride she felt initially has melted away. Her identity is reduced to an accent.

During a staff meeting, Elena, one of the young new teachers on staff, shares her innovative idea for integrating technology into the curriculum, her voice filled with excitement. The room falls silent for a moment too long before a senior colleague leans forward, saying, "That's ambitious, but let's leave the tech to the IT department, shall we?" Laughter fills the room, not unkind, but dismissive. Elena's idea, once bright and promising, dims. She is pushed back to her place.

In the crowded school hallway, Lucas hears a classmate ask, "So, which one is your real mom?" The question, casual and innocent on the surface, seeps in and lingers deep inside him. Lucas shrugs, offering an explanation he's given too many times, while inside, a small part of him retreats.

———————

After a particularly exciting professional development technology conference, Mr. Thompson introduces his classroom to a new digital learning tool, eager to engage his students with the latest educational technology. During a faculty meeting, he shares his success, only to be met with a joking remark from a younger colleague: "Careful, we don't want you getting in over your head with all this high-tech stuff." Laughter follows, not malicious, but echoing a sentiment that his age might be a barrier to innovation. Mr. Thompson's smile fades slightly, his enthusiasm dampened by the gentle jab.

———————

During a literature discussion, Aisha offers an interpretation of a novel that reflects her unique cultural perspective. The teacher responds, "That's an interesting take, but let's try to stick to the more universal themes and stay away from these hot-button issues." Aisha's insight, once vibrant, and her eagerness to contribute to the richness of the discussion are quieted to preserve the comfort of the group.

———————

After scoring the winning goal in a soccer game, Oliver overhears a remark from a spectator, "Pretty fast for a big guy." The comment stings and feels like a backhanded compliment—an unspoken bias, framing his athletic success as an exception rather than a result of hard work. Oliver's moment of triumph feels tinged by the implication that he's too big to be performing the way he is.

———————

In a parent-teacher conference, Mira discusses a student's progress, suggesting strategies for improvement. The parent, nodding along, suddenly says, "You're so young; do you have kids of your own?" The question, innocent on its surface, implies that Mira's advice might lack validity without personal parenting experience. Mira's professional expertise, built on education and experience, momentarily feels undermined, her age and personal life unexpectedly pulled into the professional discussion as measures of her capability.

———————

These vignettes capture the subtle, everyday occurrences of microaggressions and more overt expressions of bias within the educational environment, based on implicit bias. They serve as reminders of the ongoing work needed to cultivate a school culture that truly values and respects the diversity of experiences, perspectives, and identities of all its members. Many of these include instances of expressed bias that may be invisible to the offenders; therefore, it is essential that we examine our own underlying biases to guard against these types of microaggressions.

Our educational environments, much like buildings, require constant attention and maintenance to ensure they stand strong. The subtle undercurrents of bias, like unnoticed cracks in a foundation, can undermine the integrity of schools. This chapter pivots toward a critical examination of bias in schools, underscoring the importance of integrating anti-biased approaches and values into the very framework of educational systems. By doing so, you can strengthen your school with policies and programs as well as a culture that inherently supports diversity, equity, and inclusion (DEI). Building such an environment is essential for nurturing a place where every student and teacher can thrive.

When I think of my own context as a White, average-income woman in Canada, I am afforded privileges many others are not. When it comes to bias, I have many blind spots. Although my background wasn't perfect, and I've experienced poverty, a less than ideal upbringing, and significant adversity throughout my life, I was blessed with the support of a close-knit community on Gabriola Island and have a deep network of loving family and friends, opportunities, and comforts, which are all privileges. I recognize that the world I experience is not the same for everyone, and my position has been shaped, in part, by systemic inequities and biases that have favored me over others.

Though I may not have chosen this privilege, I have benefited from it—and with that comes a responsibility to listen, learn, and seek to understand the experiences of those who have walked different paths. I humbly acknowledge that I still have so much to learn about the complexities of the world and the inequalities within it. My commitment is to continue educating myself, challenge my biases, and leverage my privilege to advocate for a more equitable and inclusive world for all, which is why this chapter is such an important element of the belonging conversation.

Implicit bias is a significant barrier to creating a culture of belonging in schools. Biases can negatively impact student and staff experiences, lead to discrimination and exclusion, and hinder the development of inclusive practices (Newkirk, 2019). Belonging is closely linked to issues of equity, diversity, and inclusion, as creating a sense of belonging involves recognizing and valuing the unique backgrounds and experiences of all individuals within a community (Newkirk, 2019).

This chapter is about uncovering those hidden influences that may unwittingly shape attitudes and behaviors, limiting your capacity to foster true inclusivity and belonging. You will gain tools to identify, confront, and mitigate your own biases, ensuring they do not inhibit the welcoming, equitable environment you strive to build.

Have you ever thought about the invisible forces that shape the way you perceive, interact, and react to the world around you? What invisible biases might lie beneath your own conscious awareness? As you read this chapter, I invite you to pause for a moment and reflect on these thought-provoking questions:

- Do you tend to gravitate toward people who look, think, or act like you? If so, why do you think this is?
- Can you recall a time when you made an assumption about someone based on their appearance, and your assumption turned out to be wrong? What impact did this realization have on you?
- Are there certain stereotypes that you've been socialized to believe about certain groups of people? How have these beliefs affected your interactions and relationships?
- Do you feel uncomfortable when your biases are challenged? What does this discomfort tell you?
- Can you identify a time when you became aware of an implicit bias you held? What steps did you take to confront and manage it?
- How do you think your biases might impact your role as an educator or leader? In what ways might they influence your expectations, teaching practices, and relationships with students?

As you reflect on these questions, you begin to shine a light on the powerful undercurrents of implicit bias.

Definitions of Equity, Diversity, and Inclusion Within the Context of Bias

In education, equity, diversity, and inclusion are foundational pillars, crucial for constructing a learning environment where everyone feels empowered and valued. This section lays the groundwork for understanding how, brick by brick, schools can build spaces that champion belonging, respect, and achievement for all. *Equity* involves ensuring that all individuals have access to the resources and opportunities they need to succeed, regardless of their background or identity (Newkirk, 2019). Gay's (2018) research shows that addressing issues of equity in schools is essential for promoting a sense of belonging among students from diverse backgrounds. Schools can promote equity by addressing inequities in funding, providing resources to support underrepresented students, and ensuring all students have access to high-quality instruction (Darling-Hammond, 2010).

Diversity is the difference that exists among individuals, including differences in race, ethnicity, gender, religion, and sexual orientation (Newkirk, 2019). Promoting diversity in schools is essential for creating a sense of belonging among students (Hurtado, Alvarez, Guillermo-Wann, Cuellar, & Arellano, 2012). Schools can promote diversity by implementing culturally responsive teaching practices, incorporating diverse perspectives and voices into the curriculum, and providing opportunities for students to learn about and celebrate different cultures and identities (Ladson-Billings, 2014).

Inclusion involves creating a welcoming and supportive environment that values and respects the unique perspectives and experiences of *all* individuals. Gloria Ladson-Billings (2014) writes that promoting inclusion in schools is essential for creating a sense of belonging among students from diverse backgrounds. Schools can promote inclusion by creating a culture of respect and understanding, addressing bias and discrimination, and providing support and resources for students who may feel marginalized (Ladson-Billings, 2014). Creating an inclusive school culture requires deliberate actions and sustained commitment that often fall into the following categories.

- **Culturally responsive teaching:** This pedagogical approach recognizes and respects the diverse cultural backgrounds of students, which helps make learning more relevant and engaging for all students. Recognizing and respecting diverse cultural backgrounds in teaching practices align with Ladson-Billings's (2014) emphasis on culturally relevant pedagogy.

- **Professional development on bias and inclusion:** Provide ongoing training and professional development for teachers and staff to help them recognize and address their own biases, understand the importance of inclusion, and develop strategies to create an inclusive classroom environment. Sylvia Hurtado and colleagues (2012) highlight the importance of training teachers to recognize and address their biases and understand inclusion.

- **Inclusive curricular design:** Develop a curriculum that reflects the diversity of the world outside the classroom, incorporating materials and resources that represent a variety of cultures, histories, and perspectives (Ladson-Billings, 2014).

- **Student voice and agency:** Hurtado and colleagues (2012) suggest empowering students by giving them a voice in decisions that affect their learning and school life, with student-led conferences, representation on school committees, and opportunities for students to lead initiatives or projects.

- **Safe and supportive spaces:** Establish safe spaces within the school where students can share their experiences and feelings through counseling services, peer support groups, or designated safe zones for marginalized students (Ladson-Billings, 2014).

- **Anti-bullying policies and programs:** Implement strong anti-bullying policies and programs that specifically address bias and discrimination (Ladson-Billings, 2014).

- **Community and family engagement:** Foster a strong connection between the school and the wider community, including students' families. This can involve community-based learning projects, multicultural events, and workshops for families on supporting inclusion at home (Hurtado et al., 2012).

- **Accessibility:** Ensure that the school environment is physically and digitally accessible to all students, including those with disabilities (Ladson-Billings, 2014).

- **Restorative justice practices:** Adopt restorative justice practices to address conflicts and misconduct, as suggested by Hurtado and colleagues (2012). These practices focus on repairing harm and restoring relationships rather than punishment, promoting a more inclusive and understanding school culture. (I explore this concept in the next chapter.)

- **Diverse human resources and staff recruitment:** Strive for diverse teaching and administrative staff that reflect the student population. This helps provide role models for students and ensures a variety of perspectives within the school community (Hurtado et al., 2012).

- **Social-emotional learning programs:** Incorporate SEL into the curriculum to help students develop empathy, resilience, and social awareness. These skills are crucial for fostering an inclusive environment where students respect and understand each other (Binfet, 2022).

Implementing these strategies requires a coordinated effort across the entire school community. By prioritizing inclusion, schools can create a culture of respect and understanding that benefits all students.

All students require a sense of belonging to learn effectively, and this is particularly vital in the context of equity, diversity, and inclusion (Hurtado et al., 2012). Students who are frequently subjected to negative racial and ethnic stereotypes—including but not limited to African American, Latino/a, Native American, and Asian American students—encounter a unique challenge in achieving this sense of belonging (Murphy & Zirkel, 2015).

Stigma refers to the negative labels and discrimination faced by individuals and groups that can have a deleterious effect on their self-concept and overall well-being (Murphy & Zirkel, 2015). As noted previously, stereotype threat suggests that some students may grapple with heightened uncertainty and anxiety about their place in academic environments, especially when they feel at risk of conforming to stereotypes about their group (Murphy & Zirkel, 2015). Stigma and stereotype threat can disproportionately impact their academic performance compared to their White peers. Therefore, fostering an educational setting that promotes equity and inclusion is essential. Acknowledge and deliberately address these varied racial and ethnic experiences to ensure all students have an equitable opportunity to belong and succeed academically (Murphy & Zirkel, 2015).

The Meaning of Bias

First, it's essential to understand the meaning of bias. *Bias* refers to the inclination or prejudice for or against one person or group, especially in a way considered to be unfair (Newkirk, 2019). Biases can be based on factors such as gender, age, race, religion, nationality, sexual orientation, gender identity, ability, socioeconomic status, and more. They are often subconscious, formed through experiences and societal conditioning. Encourage staff and students to reflect on their own biases through self-assessment tools and exercises.

- Start by educating staff on what biases are and how they can affect decision making and interactions.
- Set aside time in staff meetings for open discussions about personal biases and experiences.

- Encourage staff to take online tests like the Harvard Implicit Association Test (IAT; https://implicit.harvard.edu/implicit/takeatest.html) to identify their own unconscious biases.
- Provide resources for further learning and reflection on biases, such as articles, podcasts, or books.

Recognizing that everyone has biases is the first step toward addressing them. Allowing opportunities to explore bias within psychologically safe spaces is essential to fostering a culture of belonging in schools. The following is a list of recommended resources that educators and leaders can reference to learn more about bias, inclusion, and diversity.

Podcasts

- *Teaching While White*: This podcast seeks to move the conversation forward on how to be consciously, intentionally antiracist in the classroom. It includes discussions with educators and experts about the issues of race and the impact on teaching.
- *Code Switch*: This NPR podcast is hosted by journalists of color and tackles the subject of race head-on. It explores how race impacts every part of society—from politics and pop culture to history, sports, and everything in between.

Books

- *How to Be an Antiracist* **by Ibram X. Kendi (2019):** This book provides a groundbreaking approach to understanding and uprooting racism and inequality in society—and in ourselves.
- *Culturally Responsive Teaching and the Brain* **by Zaretta Hammond (2015):** This book offers a practical framework for designing and implementing culturally responsive instruction. It's filled with examples, activities, and insights that can help educators engage ethnically and culturally diverse students.
- *Blindspot: Hidden Biases of Good People* **by Mahzarin R. Banaji and Anthony G. Greenwald (2013):** This book delves into the hidden biases we all carry from a lifetime of experiences with social groups—age, gender, race, ethnicity, religion, social class, sexuality, disability status, or nationality.

- ***The Guide for White Women Who Teach Black Boys* by Eddie Moore Jr., Ali Michael, and Marguerite W. Penick-Parks (2018):** This book bridges the gap between good intentions and meaningful change. It combines essays from prominent voices in the field of education and provides practical tools and techniques for educators.

Articles

- **"White Privilege: Unpacking the Invisible Knapsack" by Peggy McIntosh (1989):** This classic article on White privilege and racial inequality remains a useful tool for educators to understand their own biases and the systemic structures in place.

- **"'Why Are All the Black Kids Still Sitting Together in the Cafeteria?'" by Beverly Daniel Tatum (2017):** This article, which examines recent events since Tatum's (1997) classic book, is a text that discusses the psychology of racism and how it affects the actions and perceptions of both students and educators.

Resource

- **The National SEED (Seeking Educational Equity and Diversity) Project:** This resource (www.nationalseedproject.org) helps teachers and community members create their own local, yearlong, peer-led SEED seminars in which participants use their own experiences and those of their students, children, and colleagues to widen and deepen school and college curricula and make communities more inclusive.

A Reveal of the Unseen

Begin by considering implicit bias as the unconscious beliefs or attitudes toward certain groups of people that can influence your actions or decisions in an automatic and unconscious manner. These biases are usually not products of malicious intent but are universal and reside in everyone, subtly influencing behavior (Newkirk, 2019).

Researchers at Harvard University involved with Project Implicit (n.d.) created the Implicit Association Test. You can access this test using the featured QR code. This influential study has revolutionized the understanding of biases, helping people recognize that they are not just explicit, conscious prejudices, but can also be implicit and unseen. This test uses reaction times to measure automatic associations between social categories and evaluative words. Imagine the IAT as a mirror that shows how people sometimes unknowingly lean toward certain preferences or beliefs.

In a school, this could be like a history teacher mostly talking about European events without realizing they're missing out on stories from other parts of the world. By using this mirror, teachers can better see these unintentional omissions and work to include a wider range of perspectives in their lessons.

It is worth mentioning that there is a fine line between cultural appropriation and cultural appreciation. *Cultural appropriation* is taking elements from another culture without understanding or respect, potentially perpetuating stereotypes. In contrast, *cultural appreciation* is about genuinely valuing and learning about another culture's practices with respect and acknowledgment, without claiming them as one's own. Essentially, while appropriation can diminish or misrepresent, appreciation seeks to honor.

A Safe Environment for All

Fostering an environment where staff, students, and family members feel safe to discuss and confront their biases is essential. Encouraging an open, nonjudgmental environment where everyone feels comfortable sharing their experiences and perspectives is also essential, but it is important to acknowledge that conversations about bias can be challenging in educational settings. When educators and school leaders approach these discussions, they often encounter a myriad of challenges, such as defensiveness, discomfort, fear of misspeaking or simply saying the wrong thing, and the emotional intensity that such dialogues may elicit (Singleton & Linton, 2006).

To foster an environment conducive to open and constructive discussions, it is crucial to establish ground rules that promote respect, active listening, and confidentiality (Singleton & Linton, 2006). Leaders should educate themselves on the complex issues of bias and systemic inequality to navigate these conversations with informed confidence (DiAngelo, 2018). Structured activities, such as the Harvard Implicit Association Test, can serve as tools to objectively examine personal biases within a safe setting (Project Implicit, n.d.).

Encouraging personal reflection helps participants articulate their experiences in a space that mitigates the fear of judgment (DiAngelo, 2018). Incorporating external resources, such as scholarly articles, podcasts, and books, can offer a solid foundation for discussion and provide diverse perspectives (Kendi, 2019). Leaders can further ease the intimidation of these conversations by sharing their own experiences with bias, thereby modeling vulnerability and openness (Brown, 2018).

The role of the facilitator is important as well. By guiding rather than leading the conversation and asking open-ended questions, educators can create a more inclusive dialogue (Singleton & Linton, 2006). Recognizing and managing emotions as they arise are also key components of these discussions, ensuring that participants feel heard and supported (Chandler-Ward, Denevi, & Talusan, 2017). It is also beneficial to establish this dialogue as an ongoing part of the school culture (Hammond, 2015). Concluding with actionable steps allows participants to apply their insights and contribute to creating an inclusive environment (Chandler-Ward et al., 2017).

The endeavor to discuss bias within schools is a necessary step toward cultivating an anti-bias education. By approaching these conversations with careful planning, empathy, and a commitment to ongoing dialogue, educators can lead by example and steer their institutions toward greater equity and inclusion.

A few tips to keep in mind when creating a psychologically safe environment, inspired by Kendi (2019), include the following.

- Cultivate an open, nonjudgmental school culture where staff, students, and stakeholders can freely express their thoughts and concerns through vulnerability and modeling.
- Encourage open discussions about biases and their impacts.
- Establish clear channels (like an anonymous suggestion box or a designated person) where staff and students can raise concerns related to bias.
- Address reported concerns promptly and transparently.

The following sections address specific strategies schools can use to ensure a safe, welcoming environment as free from bias as possible.

Bolster Diversity and Inclusion

Promoting diversity and inclusion in the workplace can help combat biases. This could involve implementing diverse hiring practices, celebrating multicultural events throughout the year, or setting up mentorship programs to support underrepresented groups (Newkirk, 2019).

- Implement diverse hiring practices at the district level, including blind recruitment processes or targeted recruitment drives for underrepresented groups.

- Celebrate diversity in your school by acknowledging and participating in multicultural events or holidays, paying special attention to all the various holidays individuals in your building celebrate, as well as consistently adopting an environment that honors and values diversity all year.

- Set up mentorship or buddy programs that support diversity.

Encourage Staff to Embrace the Perspectives of Others

Promote perspective-taking exercises that encourage staff to step into the shoes of their colleagues, particularly those from diverse backgrounds (Zaidi, 2022). This fosters empathy and understanding, and challenges preconceived biases.

- Integrate perspective-taking exercises into team-building activities or bias-training workshops.

- Promote a culture of empathy and understanding by encouraging staff to understand and appreciate their colleagues' experiences and viewpoints.

- Encourage employees to share their experiences and backgrounds, promoting understanding and empathy among the team.

Remain Accountable

Implement accountability measures to ensure that combating bias is not a one-time event but an ongoing process (Newkirk, 2019). This could involve periodic bias training, follow-up discussions, or incorporating diversity and inclusion goals into performance evaluations.

Efforts to dismantle bias in educational settings demand ongoing, systemic action. It's not enough to address bias with sporadic initiatives; anti-bias efforts must be woven into the very fabric of the institution's daily routines and values. The following strategies have proven effective to systemic change as it relates to anti-bias efforts.

- **Regular bias training:** Implementing regular, mandatory training sessions for staff can keep the principles of equity and inclusion in focus (Sue, 2015).

- **Ongoing professional development:** Providing workshops and seminars focused on diversity and inclusion for professional development can ensure these concepts are consistently reinforced (Gay, 2018).

- **Performance metrics:** Incorporating diversity and inclusion goals into performance evaluations with clear, measurable outcomes can help maintain accountability (Kendi, 2019).

- **Feedback mechanisms:** Establishing a system for anonymous reporting allows individuals to voice concerns about bias, ensuring that school leaders can address these issues promptly and effectively (Okun, 2010).

- **Curriculum audits:** Regular curriculum reviews can ensure that teaching materials reflect a multitude of perspectives and actively work against perpetuating stereotypes (Ladson-Billings, 2014).

- **Inclusion committees:** Creating committees dedicated to equity efforts, representing a diverse cross section of the school community, can foster a shared responsibility for inclusion (Tatum, 2017).

- **Student-led initiatives:** Supporting initiatives led by students encourages a sense of ownership and agency in building a more inclusive school environment (Pollock, 2017).

- **Transparent reporting:** An annual diversity and inclusion report can provide transparency and track progress toward the school's stated goals (Newkirk, 2019).

These strategies, when combined, represent a robust approach to addressing bias. They move schools from a reactive stance to a proactive and strategic one, addressing bias when it occurs but also working to prevent it.

Case studies are invaluable because they offer a glimpse into the *how* of implementing such measures, allowing educators to learn from the successes and challenges experienced by others. The next section presents a series of case studies showcasing how various educational institutions have embedded anti-bias strategies into their culture, yielding some impressive and tangible results.

Case Studies of Inclusive and Diverse Schools

Many schools across the United States and Canada are working to build a positive and bias-free culture in support of all students and staff. Exploring diversity, equity, and inclusion initiatives in K–12 public schools reveals various strategies and outcomes. Sometimes these ideals may seem out of reach, but the following case studies demonstrate how these efforts can provide actionable examples for district leadership teams, principals, and educators.

High Tech High School, San Diego, California

This institution adopts project-based learning that incorporates students' diverse experiences and interests into real-world projects. By doing so, it enhances academic engagement as well as promotes unity and respect among students from varied backgrounds (Berger, Rugen, & Woodfin, 2014).

- **Actionable strategy:** Implement interdisciplinary projects that allow students to explore their identities and backgrounds, fostering a collaborative learning environment.

- **Project-based learning incorporating diversity:** Create interdisciplinary projects that require students to explore and present their cultural backgrounds, interests, and experiences. This could involve implementing community research projects, creating digital stories, or designing solutions to local problems that reflect the students' diverse perspectives.

- **Professional development on project-based learning:** Organize professional development workshops on designing and implementing project-based learning that reflects student diversity and fosters collaboration among students from varied backgrounds.

Harvey Milk High School, New York, New York

Named after the iconic gay rights activist, this school provides a nurturing environment for LGBTQ+ students through a curriculum that celebrates their identities, promoting acceptance and pride (Kosciw, Greytak, Bartkiewicz, Boesen, & Palmer, 2012).

- **Actionable strategy:** Develop and integrate curriculum content that highlights the contributions and histories of LGBTQ+ individuals and communities.

- **Curriculum development:** Create a curriculum that includes literature, historical events, and contributions of LGBTQ+ individuals and communities. This might include guest speakers from the LGBTQ+ community and partnerships with LGBTQ+ organizations to provide resources and support.

- **Safe space training:** Provide safe space training for all staff and students, focusing on understanding LGBTQ+ issues, combating discrimination, and promoting a supportive environment.

Indian Community School, Franklin, Wisconsin

Indian Community School integrates Indigenous cultures, traditions, and languages into its curriculum, strengthening students' cultural identity and sense of belonging (Demmert, 2001).

- **Actionable strategy:** Involve community elders and incorporate traditional knowledge and practices into the curriculum to enrich students' understanding of their heritage.

- **Cultural integration in curriculum:** Integrate Indigenous cultures, languages, and traditions into the curriculum through storytelling, traditional arts, and language courses. Collaborate with local Indigenous communities to bring in guest speakers, elders, and cultural practitioners who can enrich students' learning experiences.

- **Cultural awareness professional development:** Facilitate professional development sessions for staff on Indigenous cultures and histories, culturally responsive teaching practices, and strategies for integrating cultural traditions into everyday learning.

Burnaby School District, Burnaby, British Columbia

This district offers professional development programs aimed at combating homophobia and transphobia, thereby creating a more inclusive environment for LGBTQ+ students (Taylor & Peter, 2011).

- **Actionable strategy:** Conduct regular training sessions for staff on LGBTQ+ inclusivity and anti-bullying strategies to foster a supportive school climate.

- **Professional development on LGBTQ+ inclusivity:** Offer regular professional development sessions for teachers and staff on LGBTQ+ inclusivity, anti-bullying strategies, and understanding the challenges LGBTQ+ students face.

- **Policy review and guidelines:** Review existing policies to ensure they are inclusive of LGBTQ+ students, develop guidelines for supporting transgender and nonbinary students, and implement procedures for addressing instances of homophobia and transphobia.

Skyline High School, Ann Arbor, Michigan

The Speak Out program, led by LGBTQ+ students, offers anti-bullying training for students and staff, empowering students to contribute to a culture of inclusivity (Kosciw et al., 2012).

- **Actionable strategy:** Support student-led initiatives that promote diversity and inclusivity, providing platforms for students to lead conversations and training on anti-bullying and inclusivity.

- **Student-led initiatives:** Encourage and support the creation of student-led groups, such as genders and sexualities alliances (GSAs) or diversity councils, that can organize events, discussions, and training sessions on inclusivity and anti-bullying.

- **Empowerment through leadership:** Provide leadership training and resources to students leading these initiatives, enabling them to effectively plan and execute programs that promote a culture of inclusivity.

Toronto District School Board, Toronto, Ontario

Committed to inclusivity, this district engages in professional development on antiracism, religious accommodation, and a curriculum reflecting student identities (James & Turner, 2017).

- **Actionable strategy:** Develop and implement comprehensive professional development programs on antiracism and cultural competency for all staff members.

- **Antiracism professional development:** The district can provide comprehensive training for all staff on antiracism, cultural competency, and addressing biases, with specific actions and strategies for creating an inclusive classroom environment.

- **Inclusive curriculum review:** Conduct a thorough review of the curriculum across subjects to ensure it reflects the diverse identities of students, includes antiracism education, and promotes understanding and respect for all cultures.

Chicago Public Schools Office of Student Protections and Title IX

Chicago Public Schools has launched a multifaceted approach to foster inclusion and belonging across its schools. Key efforts include the following.

Equity Office

Focused on addressing disparities in funding and resources, the equity office implements programs aimed at supporting underrepresented students. These include mentoring and tutoring, specifically designed to elevate those who have traditionally been marginalized.

- **Actionable strategy:** Schools can replicate this by conducting thorough audits of resource allocation and establishing targeted support programs based on identified needs.

- **Principals and teachers:** Identify and track the performance and participation of underrepresented students in advanced courses, extracurricular activities, and support programs. Develop targeted intervention programs, such as peer mentoring and tutoring, that cater specifically to the needs of these students.

- **School district:** Allocate funds and resources to schools with higher populations of underrepresented students, ensuring equitable access to technology, learning materials, and extracurricular opportunities.

Office of Language and Cultural Education

This office ensures that diverse learners receive the necessary resources and support to succeed. It champions a curriculum that is both culturally responsive and inclusive, acknowledging the unique backgrounds of all students.

- **Actionable strategy:** To adopt a similar approach, develop curricula that incorporate students' cultural histories and languages, and provide professional development for teachers on cultural competency.

- **Principals:** Collaborate with local cultural organizations and communities to bring cultural education and language programs into the school, enhancing the curriculum with multicultural perspectives.

- **Teachers:** Integrate cultural studies into the curriculum across subjects. Use culturally relevant teaching materials and methods that reflect the diverse backgrounds of students.

Office of Social-Emotional Learning

With a focus on enhancing the school climate and promoting students' well-being, this office integrates SEL across the district.

- **Actionable strategy:** Implementing comprehensive SEL programs districtwide can help other schools create supportive environments conducive to learning and personal growth.

- **Schools:** Implement schoolwide SEL programs that include professional development for teachers on SEL strategies, classroom activities that promote emotional intelligence, and school policies that support a positive school climate.

- **Teachers:** Regularly incorporate SEL activities into the classroom, such as mindfulness exercises, emotion regulation strategies, and collaborative problem-solving tasks.

These case studies demonstrate some of the accessible approaches many schools are taking to integrate DEI into their curricula and policies. From professional development and literacy programs to culturally responsive pedagogy, these efforts are pivotal in creating inclusive educational environments where all students can thrive. By implementing initiatives that promote equity, diversity, and inclusion, schools can create a more supportive and inclusive environment that promotes student success and well-being.

The following Classroom Toolbox and School Leadership Toolbox sections strive to equip educators and school leaders with the strategies and tools needed to foster a supportive and bias-free environment in their schools.

CLASSROOM TOOLBOX

> By focusing on the BUILD elements—boundaries, understanding, integrity, listening, and dependability—teachers can use these activities to encourage and promote inclusive and bias-free classrooms and schools.

Five Key Questions: Inclusive Classroom Resource Filter

⊘ Boundaries, 🤝 Integrity

To design lessons that are not only memorable and effective, but also inclusive and representative of the students in their classrooms, educators can filter lessons, resources, and materials through the following set of questions. These questions address the concepts of representation, accessibility, inclusivity, equity, and critical thinking, and serve to assess classroom resources and lessons for alignment with diversity, inclusion, and equity ideals.

Use the questions to determine whether to include an activity, resource, or lesson methodology within your practice, considering the context of your classroom community. For example, before reading a particular book to your second-grade class, consider whether the characters represent your students. Can everyone access the content, or do you need to adapt some of the vocabulary to facilitate comprehension? Can students see themselves in the plot situations and characters? Are stereotypes present? Are the characters represented in an equitable manner? Does the book reinforce stereotypes, or does it require the reader to "think outside of the box"?

While not every resource will check off every box, these five questions provide a helpful filter through which to consider the resources you introduce to students.

1. **Representation: Who's in the room?** Does this material reflect the diversity of the world around you, including people from different backgrounds, cultures, and experiences?
2. **Accessibility: Can everyone climb aboard?** Is this content accessible and understandable to all students, regardless of their abilities, learning styles, or language proficiency?
3. **Inclusivity: Does every voice matter?** Does the lesson ensure every student feels valued and included, without fear of being marginalized or stereotyped?

4. **Equity: Is the playing field level?** Does this resource examine and mitigate biases, ensuring all students have equitable opportunities to succeed and be heard? Are there aspects of the resource, lesson, or activity that reinforce inequities?

5. **Critical thinking and reflection: Are we thinking and growing?** Does the material challenge students to think critically about diversity, equity, and inclusion, and reflect on their own perspectives and biases?

These questions are designed to be straightforward and engaging, encouraging educators to quickly assess the extent to which their classroom resources and lessons align with diversity, inclusion, and equity ideals. They can help educators remember to apply these important considerations in their teaching practices.

Tech Tips

🤝 Integrity, 🛡️ Dependability, 🤲 Understanding

Creating a safe space where students feel valued, understood, and free to express themselves authentically is an essential aspect of building belonging (MacKenzie, 2018). Assistive and adaptive classroom responses to diversity and disability can also contribute to the experience of psychological safety. For example, leveraging assistive technologies and digital tools to tailor learning experiences for students with varied communication abilities can be a crucial example of creating safe environments for all children and adults. Implementing resources like text-to-speech software and interactive learning applications can make educational content more accessible and engaging for all students. This approach supports individual learning needs as well as promotes active participation in classroom activities, enhancing students' sense of achievement and belonging for those with developmental challenges and language processing exceptionalities, and English learners (Rao, Ok, & Bryant, 2014).

These technologies, when integrated into classrooms, benefit all students by fostering a more inclusive learning environment. Some key assistive technologies include the following.

- **Text-to-speech (TTS) software** aids students with reading difficulties, like dyslexia, and benefits all students by supporting multitasking with audio learning.
- **Speech-to-text (STT) software** helps students with physical or writing challenges by converting speech to text, useful for all in dictating work.

- **Audiobooks and digital textbooks** provide support for students with visual impairments or reading disorders and enhance auditory learning for others.

- **Screen readers** are crucial for students with significant visual impairments, allow access to content via speech or Braille, and are useful for auditory content consumption.

- **Graphic organizers and mind mapping tools** aid in organizing thoughts for students with executive function disorders and improve planning skills for all students.

- **Augmentative and alternative communication (AAC) devices** support speech or language challenges, promoting interaction and inclusivity in classroom activities.

- **Adjustable desks and ergonomic chairs** address physical accessibility needs and benefit all students by promoting comfort and focus.

- **Educational software and games** are accessible learning tools that cater to diverse needs, engaging all students in fun, interactive skill practice.

These technologies cater to specific disabilities but also enrich the learning experience for all students, underlining the importance of a universally designed learning environment. Thinking through the lens of Universal Design for Learning can make learning richer for all students.

Empowering Student-Led Special Interest Groups

Listening, Understanding

Creating special interest–inclusive groups at school can foster a sense of belonging and community among students, especially when these groups are built on principles of diversity, inclusion, and equity. Consider the following step-by-step approach to support students in establishing special interest groups.

1. **Be responsive and identify students' interests and needs:** Facilitate open discussions to identify students' interests and needs, encouraging them to express what kinds of groups they feel are missing or needed in the school community. This might happen in the classroom through a structured lesson, through ad hoc discussions in the lunchroom or hallways, and through casual conversations as they arise. This step reinforces the importance of being deeply connected to your students.

2. **Help students make a plan:** Have students draft a proposal for their group, outlining its purpose, goals, and how it promotes inclusivity. This includes a plan for meetings, activities, and how to welcome new members.

3. **Seek administrative approval:** Submit the proposal to school administration for approval, ensuring it aligns with school policies and values, highlighting the group's commitment to inclusivity and diversity.

4. **Invite others:** Launch a recruitment drive using school announcements, posters, and social media, emphasizing the group's open and inclusive nature. Ensure the messaging is welcoming to all, regardless of background or experience with the interest.

5. **Host the first meeting:** Organize the first meeting with activities that allow members to get to know each other, set group norms that uphold inclusivity, and discuss plans for future meetings and activities.

6. **Establish inclusivity norms:** Develop a charter or set of norms that all members agree on to ensure the group remains inclusive, supportive, and respectful of all members' voices and identities.

7. **Implement regular activities and reflection:** Conduct regular meetings and activities, ensuring they are accessible and engaging for all members. Periodically reflect on the group's inclusivity and adjust as needed.

The following are some examples of possible school groups.

- **Coding club for all skill levels:** Students interested in coding span various skill levels, and beginners might feel intimidated. Encourage the founding members to structure the club with mentorship roles, pairing more experienced coders with beginners to foster a supportive learning environment.

- **Multicultural book club:** Ensure representation of various cultures and avoid the dominance of any single perspective. Assist students in creating a diverse book selection committee and planning events that celebrate and discuss each culture represented in the books.

- **Genders and sexualities alliances:** It can be challenging to create a safe and welcoming space for LGBTQ+ students and allies in a school with varying levels of acceptance. Work with students to establish clear confidentiality norms, plan inclusive events, and provide resources for education and support within the group.

- **Environmental club with a focus on local action:** Balance diverse interests within environmental activism and ensure actionable projects. Help students brainstorm project ideas that have tangible impacts, such as a school recycling program or community garden, ensuring roles and responsibilities are clearly defined and inclusive.

- **Anti-bias workshop series:** Some students may not be aware of their own biases or how these biases can affect their peers. Assist students in organizing a series of workshops focusing on anti-bias education. Each session could be led by a different student group or external facilitator, covering topics like unconscious bias, stereotypes, and how to be an ally.

- **Antiracism book and film club:** Racism and racial injustice are prevalent issues in society, and students may want to create a space to explore these topics through literature and cinema, but it can be challenging to ensure respectful and productive discussions. Help students develop a diverse and representative list of books and films, as well as guidelines for discussion that encourage open, respectful dialogue. Facilitate training or preparation sessions for moderators to ensure they are equipped to handle sensitive topics and manage discussions effectively.

- **Support group for students with disabilities:** Research underscores the importance of peer support and collaborative learning in enhancing the educational experience for students with disabilities, promoting both academic success and social inclusion (Tan, Schwab, & Perren, 2022). Students with disabilities may feel isolated or underrepresented in school activities. A support group not only provides support and advocacy but also raises awareness among the wider student body.

  Support students in creating a group that serves as both a safe space for students with disabilities and a platform for advocacy on accessibility issues. This group could organize awareness campaigns, guest speaker events, and workshops on topics such as inclusivity, accessibility, and the rights of individuals with disabilities.

In each of these scenarios, the key support strategy involves guiding students to ensure their initiatives are inclusive and educational, and promote a culture of respect and understanding. By providing frameworks, resources, and encouragement, educators can empower students to lead meaningful change and foster a more inclusive school environment.

Diversity and Inclusion Partnerships With Community Organizations

Integrity, Dependability

Schools can foster partnerships with community organizations and resources to help support students. It can feel overwhelming to create these partnerships due to lack of access when researching or choosing a particular cause, or because of not knowing where to start. To connect your classroom or student body with local businesses, nonprofits, and other organizations that support and reinforce diversity, inclusion, and equity through their policies and projects, some ideas to make the process easier and less intimidating follow.

- Consider partnerships with local chapters of national organizations like the Rotary Club, which often supports educational and community initiatives, or local nonprofits focused on community service.

- Consider accessing digital tools to establish partnerships with organizations beyond the local community. Online platforms like Pathful (www.pathful.com) connect classrooms with industry professionals virtually, allowing students to engage with diverse perspectives and experiences.

- Programs like 4-H, which is deeply rooted in rural communities, often provide leadership training and community service opportunities that align with leadership goals.

- Integrate cultural awareness into the school curriculum through events, projects, and guest speakers. The National Education Association (NEA) offers resources for educators to develop inclusive curriculum plans and organize school events that celebrate diversity.

Before engaging with a particular organization, consider the following questions to determine whether it is the right fit for your school or classroom.

- What specific needs of our student body can this organization help address?

- What resources (for example, time, expertise, funding) can the organization offer, and how do these complement our school's resources?

- How accessible is the organization for collaboration with the school (considering location, communication, and willingness)?

- Can the organization provide educational support, programs, learning experiences, or opportunities to promote student involvement, leadership, and learning?
- Does the organization represent or serve diverse groups within the community?
- Is there potential for a long-term partnership that could grow and evolve with the school's diversity and inclusion initiatives?

These resources and questions provide a scaffold for educators to build inclusive educational environments in areas where resources may not be readily apparent but are nonetheless present and accessible.

Multigrade Lessons for Teaching About Implicit Bias

Understanding

Teachers can use the following lessons to help teach students the concept of implicit bias across three grade-level spans (grades K–2, grades 3–5, and middle school to high school).

We Are All Unique: Lesson for Grades K–2 Students

Objective: Students will learn about implicit bias and how it can affect their classmates and the broader community within the school.

Materials

- Picture books that depict diverse characters, such as *The Skin You Live In* by Michael Tyler (2005) and *All Are Welcome* by Alexandra Penfold (2018) (See the following additional book suggestions, page 104.)
- Whiteboard or chart paper
- Markers
- Index cards or sticky notes
- Writing utensils

Steps for the Lesson

1. **Introduce the topic (ten minutes):** Select and read a storybook that features characters from diverse backgrounds.
    a. Ask students if they noticed anything about the characters in the book.

b. Ask them if they have ever felt left out or different from others.

c. Explain that sometimes people make judgments about others based on how they look, their skin color, or where they come from without even realizing it. This is called *implicit bias*.

d. Consider some of the following additional book suggestions.

> *The Day You Begin* by Jacqueline Woodson (2018): This book offers a sensitive portrayal of what it feels like to be an outsider, touching on themes of implicit bias and the importance of embracing one's own and others' differences.

> *Strictly No Elephants* by Lisa Mantchev (2015): This is a heartwarming book about friendship and acceptance, and recognizing the fact that differences make people unique. The story provides a gentle introduction to the idea of implicit bias.

> *We're Different, We're the Same* by Bobbi Jane Kates (1992): This *Sesame Street* book is an engaging way to teach children about diversity. It showcases that, although we may look different on the outside, we're very much the same on the inside, tackling implicit bias in a subtle and age-appropriate way.

2. **Brainstorm (five minutes):** Write the words *left out* on a whiteboard or chart paper. Ask students what they think it means and record their contributions on the whiteboard or chart paper.

3. **Discuss (ten minutes):**

    a. Ask students to share examples of situations in which they felt left out, without mentioning names. Or ask them to share when they have seen it happen to someone else. Write down or share their ideas.

    b. Ask students why they think someone might feel left out. Discuss the concept of implicit bias by talking about the following concepts.

    > Sometimes, we can leave someone out when we decide something about them quickly without really knowing them.

    > Sometimes, we have thoughts that are unfair about others, based on how they look or seem to us without knowing them.

    > Sometimes, we might have ideas about people that are in the back of our minds and might not be nice.

c. Discuss with students the importance of treating others with kindness and respect, regardless of how they look or where they come from. Explain that everyone has implicit biases and that it's important to recognize them and work to overcome them.

4. **Reflect (ten minutes):** Ask students to reflect on their own biases. Distribute index cards or sticky notes. Invite students to draw a picture of themselves and write one thing they like about themselves. Then ask them to draw a picture of someone who looks different from them and write one thing they like about that person.

5. **Close (ten minutes):** Collect the index cards or sticky notes and display them in the classroom. Remind students that everyone is unique and special in their own way. Encourage them to be mindful of their implicit biases and to treat everyone with kindness and respect.

Extension Activity

You can extend this lesson by incorporating more storybooks featuring diverse characters and having students engage in group activities that promote understanding and empathy toward others.

What Is Implicit Bias? Lesson for Grades 3–5 Students

Objective: Students will learn about implicit bias and how it can affect their classmates and the broader community within the school.

Materials

- Whiteboard or chalkboard
- Markers or chalk
- Handout with scenarios depicting implicit bias (one per student)
- Writing utensils

Steps for the Lesson

1. **Introduce the topic (ten minutes):** Begin the lesson by asking students if they have ever heard the term *implicit bias*. Write the term on the board and explain that implicit bias is a type of bias that people have without realizing it. Ask students if they can think of any examples of implicit bias they have observed or experienced. Write their responses on the board.

2. **Define implicit bias (ten minutes):** Explain to students that *implicit bias* refers to attitudes or stereotypes that affect their understanding, actions, and decisions in an unconscious manner. Ask them to brainstorm different groups against which people may have implicit biases, such as people of different races, religions, genders, or abilities. Write their responses on the board.

3. **Identify examples of implicit bias (fifteen minutes):** Distribute the handout with scenarios depicting implicit bias. Have students read the scenarios and identify examples of implicit bias in each one. After they have completed the handout, ask volunteers to share their answers with the class. Use this as an opportunity to discuss why each scenario depicts implicit bias and how those biases may affect the people involved.

4. **Explore the harm of implicit bias (ten minutes):** Lead a class discussion on the harmful effects of implicit bias. Ask students how they would feel if they were the target of implicit bias, and how it might affect their ability to learn, feel safe, and belong. Use this discussion to emphasize the importance of being aware of our implicit biases and taking steps to address them.

5. **Reflect (five minutes):** Have each student write a reflection on what they learned about implicit bias during the lesson. Ask them to identify one step they can take to reduce their own implicit biases or address bias they observe in others. Collect the reflections at the end of the class.

Extension Activity

Encourage students to talk to their families about implicit bias and discuss ways they can work together to reduce implicit bias in their communities. Have them share their reflections from the lesson with their families and report back to the class on any new insights or ideas that emerged from these conversations.

Following are some scenarios based on assumptions that students could use for the activity.

- A new student in class is not good at mathematics because of their race.
- A student is not interested in science because of their gender.
- A classmate is not good at sports because of their body size.
- A student is not a good writer because of their first language.
- A classmate is not friendly because of their disability.

- A student is not a good public speaker because of their accent.
- A classmate is not artistic because of their religion.
- A student is not good at technology because of their age.
- A classmate is not a good leader because of their shyness.
- A student is not good at history because of their socioeconomic status.

You can use these scenarios to prompt discussions about implicit bias and how it can affect perceptions and actions toward others.

Exploring Implicit Bias: Lesson for Middle and High School Students

Objective: Students will learn about implicit bias and how it can affect their classmates and the broader community within the school.

Materials

- Electronic device and access to the internet
- Whiteboard or chart paper
- Markers

Steps for the Lesson

1. **Introduce the topic and discuss (ten minutes):** Introduce the concept of implicit bias to students. Explain that everyone has biases, even if they are not aware of them. Have a brief discussion about what implicit bias means and provide some examples. Ask students to share their thoughts on the topic and any experiences they may have had with implicit bias.

2. **Conduct Implicit Association Test (fifteen minutes):** Have students take an Implicit Association Test online. The IAT is a tool that measures implicit bias. You can find this tool on the Project Implicit website (https://implicit.harvard.edu/implicit/takeatest.html), hosted by Harvard University. The IAT has different tests for different topics, such as race, gender, sexuality, and age. Encourage students to take at least one test.

3. **Elicit small-group discussion (fifteen minutes):** Form groups of three to four students and ask them to discuss their IAT results. Encourage them to share their thoughts and feelings about their results and any surprises they had. Ask students to consider how their biases might impact their thoughts, and record their ideas on a whiteboard or chart paper.

4. **Offer real-life examples (ten minutes):** Provide real-life examples of implicit bias and how it can impact people's lives. This could include news stories, personal experiences, or case studies. Ask students to consider how these examples relate to their own lives and experiences.

5. **Reflect and create action plan (ten minutes):** Ask students to reflect on what they learned about implicit bias and its impact. Have them consider ways they can combat their own biases and promote equity and inclusion. Ask them to create an action plan with at least one concrete step they can take to address implicit bias in their own lives or community.

Extension Activity

Have students create bias-awareness posters to display around the school. Each poster could include a fact about implicit bias and a helpful tip (generated as a class from discussion) for recognizing and countering personal biases. This activity encourages personal autonomy, creativity, and curricular objectives related to communication, while reinforcing the lesson's concepts and promoting wider awareness within the school community.

SCHOOL LEADERSHIP TOOLBOX

> By focusing on the BUILD elements—boundaries, understanding, integrity, listening, and dependability—school leaders can use these activities to build a positive, inclusive, bias-free environment in their school.

Journal: Self-Reflection on Implicit Bias

Understanding, Integrity

Implicit bias training is not a one-time event but a continuous process of learning, reflection, and action. Tackling implicit bias is an ongoing process that demands self-awareness, introspection, and proactive steps. Through dedicated practices such as journaling, educators can embark on a path of self-examination, gaining insights into the effects of their biases and discovering effective ways to counteract them. The following is a series of journal prompts you can write about in personal journals or adapt to facilitate important discussions about bias.

- Reflect on a time when you realized your judgment or behavior was influenced by bias. How did you feel when you realized this, and what steps did or can you take to address it?
- Consider a situation in which someone else's bias affected you or someone you know. What was the impact, and how did you address the situation?
- What are three actionable steps you can take to mitigate the influence of implicit bias in your professional or personal life?
- How can you contribute to creating a more inclusive environment in your school by addressing implicit biases?

Zoom In on Implicit Bias With Your Team

Understanding, Integrity

Implicit bias exploration begins with the understanding that everyone has biases, often developed unconsciously through our environments and experiences. This foundational understanding is crucial for creating a nonjudgmental space where individuals feel comfortable exploring their biases (Banaji & Greenwald, 2013). Activities such as watching informative videos or engaging in group discussions can facilitate this understanding, setting the stage for deeper exploration. Recognizing your biases is the first step toward mitigating their impact on your actions and decisions. Through case studies and real-world scenarios, educators can see how biases affect interpersonal interactions and organizational decisions. This understanding is complemented by strategies for mitigating bias, such as practicing mindfulness, stereotype replacement, and intentional decision-making processes that account for potential biases (Lai et al., 2014).

The following activity is designed to help deepen understanding, foster empathy, and encourage exploration of implicit bias with your staff. It is structured to promote self-reflection and group discussion, which are critical components for initiating personal and collective growth toward more inclusive behaviors and practices.

Walk a Mile Exercise

Objective: To share and listen to personal stories related to bias and discrimination, deepening empathy and understanding among participants.

Directions

1. Invite participants to write a brief account of a time they experienced or witnessed bias or discrimination. Participants then share their stories anonymously by placing them in a common area, such as an online collaborative document or a simple box with slips of paper. Alternately, you can use the microaggression examples at the beginning of this chapter as discussion points.
2. Participants randomly select a story and read it aloud to the group.
3. After sharing each story, the group reflects on the emotions and biases described, discussing the impact of such experiences and how to address them.

Reflection Questions

- How did it feel to hear someone else's experience with bias?
- What are the long-term impacts of such experiences on individuals and communities?
- How can we support one another in addressing and overcoming these biases?

Follow-Up Activities

After the activity, offer powerful pathways for understanding and mitigating implicit biases in the following ways.

- **Encourage self-reflection:** Demonstrate that you value self-reflection by encouraging your team to complete the Journal: Self-Reflection on Implicit Bias activity (see page 109) to examine their biases. This ongoing process of learning and self-improvement can foster more respectful and understanding interactions with others.

- **Foster the spirit of continued education:** Encourage staff to educate themselves about different cultures, backgrounds, and experiences. This exposure can help challenge your biases and broaden your perspectives (Newkirk, 2019). Provide resources they can explore on their own.

- **Seek feedback:** Ask for feedback from diverse peers on your leadership. Encourage educators to do the same with each other. Others may notice biases you might be unaware of (Newkirk, 2019).

- **Practice mindful interactions:** Practice mindful interactions with others. Pay attention to your initial reactions and judgments and question their origins. Ask yourself whether they are based on the individual or on a stereotype or preconceived notion (Zaidi, 2022).

- **Commit to continuous learning and growth:** Challenging biases is not a one-time effort but a lifelong journey. As a staff, commit to continuing to learn, grow, and question beliefs and assumptions over time.

Remember, the goal of exploring hidden biases isn't to feel guilty or defensive, but to better understand oneself and foster more respectful and understanding interactions with others.

Bridging Perspectives

Integrity, Dependability

This strategy, from the book *Both/And Thinking* by Wendy Smith and Marianne Lewis (2022), involves exploring different viewpoints and considering the benefits and drawbacks of each. It seeks common ground and shared values, which would be easily adaptable for a staff meeting or professional development session. In education, "both/and" thinking, when talking about biases, is like telling students that there's not just one correct way to color a picture. The following are some examples.

- **Have multiple answers:** Just like some mathematics problems have more than one solution, people can have different ways of seeing or understanding something, and that's OK.

- **Value differences:** If one person thinks "this" way because of their background and another thinks "that" way, it's like preferring crayons over colored pencils. Both have value, and both can be right.

- **Break down stereotypes:** Instead of boxing people into either-or categories, such as "he's sporty" or "she's artsy," remember many people can be both. A person can be skilled at soccer *and* be a great artist; another can love cooking *and* be an avid reader.

Follow these steps to bring different perspectives into a staff meeting.

1. **Introduce the topic (five minutes):** Begin the staff meeting by introducing the concept of both/and thinking from Smith and Lewis's (2022) book. Explain how this approach encourages people to see things from multiple perspectives rather than a binary, either-or mindset.

2. **Reflect (ten minutes):** Ask participants to think of an issue or decision within the school that might have multiple valid perspectives (for example, adapting curriculum, school timings, or disciplinary policies). Ask participants to write the issue and their perspective on a note card.

3. **Pair and share (ten minutes):** Pair up participants. Each participant then shares the issue they've selected and explains their perspectives to their partners. After both participants have shared, they discuss the advantages and limitations of their viewpoints (Smith & Lewis, 2022).

Recognizing Individual Differences

Understanding, Listening

Recognizing individual differences can help create a more inclusive and equitable environment. This strategy involves acknowledging and valuing diverse backgrounds, experiences, and perspectives, and providing opportunities for personalized learning and growth (Rose, 2022). The goal of this activity is to foster an appreciation and understanding of individual differences within the staff, promoting a more inclusive and diverse school environment.

1. **Introduce the topic (ten minutes):** Talk about the importance of recognizing and celebrating differences in a collective setting and

how doing so can contribute to a more diverse, inclusive, and efficient working environment.

2. **Create personal identity maps (twenty to thirty minutes):** Each participant creates a personal identity map on a sheet of paper that they can use to represent themselves. This map should include various aspects of their identity, such as professional background, hobbies, cultural heritage, and other unique characteristics. Participants will need large sheets of construction paper or poster paper, magazines for cutting out images and text, scissors, and glue sticks.

    a. Invite participants to reflect on the different aspects of their identity, such as their job, interests, heritage, and personal traits, through a short brainstorming session.

    b. Have them look through magazines to find images, quotes, or words that resonate with these aspects of their identity.

    c. Then have them cut out their selections and arrange and glue them on large sheets of paper to create a collage that visually represents their personal identity map.

3. **Engage in sharing circles (twenty minutes):** Divide participants into small groups. Each participant shares highlights from their personal identity map, explaining the significance of the elements they've included. Encourage others to ask questions and show curiosity.

4. **Create a collective mural (fifteen minutes):** Participants post their maps on a large bulletin board or whiteboard, creating a collective mural of individual differences.

5. **Reflect (ten minutes):** Conclude with a group reflection. Discuss how this activity has illuminated the diversity within the staff, and how these differences can be a source of strength. Develop strategies on how to continue to recognize and celebrate these individual differences in the school environment.

This activity aims to create an awareness of individual differences and foster a culture of appreciation and respect. Personal identity maps serve as a visual reminder of the diversity within the staff, promoting ongoing recognition and inclusion.

Culturally Responsive Leadership

Integrity, Dependability

Create safe and welcoming spaces for BIPOC (Black, Indigenous, and people of color) and LGBTQ+ individuals by implementing inclusive language policies, displaying inclusive posters and symbols, and providing accessible and gender-neutral restrooms (National Education Association Center for Social Justice, 2021). Educating oneself on the experiences and perspectives of BIPOC and LGBTQ+ individuals through reading, attending workshops or conferences, or engaging in conversations with individuals from these communities shows dedication and commitment to inclusion and anti-bias.

The following are some steps for modeling respectful and inclusive communication and behavior among staff and students (Ladson-Billings, 2014).

- **Provide training to staff on cultural competency, communication skills, and inclusive practices:** For example, provide staff with training on cultural differences and how to address potential biases that may arise in the classroom or across the school. Staff can participate in workshops or webinars that provide strategies for creating a more inclusive educational environment.

- **Encourage staff to model respectful and inclusive behavior and language in all interactions with students and colleagues:** For example, encourage staff to use inclusive language when addressing students, avoiding language that could be perceived as discriminatory or offensive. For example, instead of saying "boys and girls," use "students," "scholars," or "class."

- **Address any incidents of disrespectful or exclusionary behavior immediately and with sensitivity:** For example, a student makes a comment about another student's religion that is offensive. Address the comment immediately and privately with the student, explaining why the comment was inappropriate and how it can be hurtful.

- **Foster opportunities for staff and students to learn about and celebrate diversity and inclusion:** Have students make presentations on influential figures and hold discussions about the impact of racial inequality and discrimination. Invite guest speakers and cultural performers to present at your school. Reinforce year-round opportunities to learn about different cultures by having students explore their history and ancestry.

- **Regularly evaluate the effectiveness of communication and behavior practices and adjust as needed:** For example, try the following strategies.
    - Conduct surveys among staff and students to assess the effectiveness of current communication and behavior practices. Gather feedback and adjust based on the survey results.
    - At the beginning of each school year, offer staff training on cultural competency and inclusive practices. Throughout the year, staff model respectful and inclusive behavior and language in all interactions with students and colleagues. When incidents of disrespectful or exclusionary behavior occur, address them immediately and with sensitivity.
    - Host cultural celebrations, such as an annual multicultural fair, and be sure teachers incorporate diverse perspectives into their curriculum.
    - At the end of each school year, staff evaluate the effectiveness of their communication and behavior practices and adjust as needed.

Bias-Free Hiring

Integrity, Dependability

Foster inclusive and equitable hiring practices by actively seeking out and recruiting diverse candidates, using inclusive job descriptions and language, and providing ongoing support and professional development for diverse staff (Cole & Mross, 2022). To help achieve your goal of fostering a diverse and inclusive educational environment, consider the following five guideposts to inform the hiring process in your school.

1. **Diverse and competent workforce:** Strive to assemble a teaching team that not only reflects the diversity of the student body but also possesses the cultural competence to effectively engage with students from various backgrounds. This includes a commitment to equity, ensuring every student can succeed.

2. **Innovation and adaptability:** Prioritize hiring educators who are innovative in their teaching approaches and adaptable to changes in educational practices and technologies. Their ability to employ diverse pedagogies will help meet students' varied learning needs.

3. **Collaboration and continuous learning:** Seek out candidates who are collaborative team players and are committed to their own professional growth. Educators who engage in ongoing learning and development can better contribute to a dynamic and evolving educational environment.

4. **Safety and feedback:** Ensure the safety of the student community through thorough background checks on all finalists for the position, while also establishing mechanisms to incorporate feedback from students, parents, and staff. This feedback is invaluable for refining hiring practices and professional development efforts.

5. **Legal and ethical compliance:** Adherence to legal standards and regulations in hiring is non-negotiable. Ensuring compliance protects the school as well as promotes a fair and equitable hiring process that supports diversity and inclusion goals.

When hiring paraprofessionals and teachers, it's crucial to assess a commitment and fluency in diversity, inclusion, and equity practices to ensure they can contribute positively to an educational environment that respects and nurtures all students' identities and backgrounds (Carnahan, 2023). The following is a list of possible interview questions designed to gauge candidates' understanding, experience, and commitment to these policies.

- Can you describe your understanding of diversity, inclusion, and equity in the educational context? How have you demonstrated a commitment to these principles in your previous roles?

- Can you share an experience in which you worked with a diverse group of students or colleagues? What challenges did you face, and how did you overcome them?

- How do you approach teaching or supporting students from different cultural, socioeconomic, and linguistic backgrounds than your own?

- Can you give an example of how you have modified your teaching strategies to accommodate the needs of all students, including those with disabilities?

- How have you pursued professional development opportunities related to diversity, equity, and inclusion?

By focusing on these key areas, schools and districts can enhance their hiring practices to create an educational environment that values diversity, supports equity, and encourages excellence in teaching and learning.

Conclusion

Confronting and addressing bias is not a quick fix but a continuous journey that requires ongoing commitment from all levels of the organization. It involves fostering self-awareness, creating a safe and inclusive environment, encouraging perspective taking, and implementing accountability measures. With these strategies, schools can begin to mitigate the effects of bias, fostering a more inclusive and fairer environment for all.

Addressing bias within a school is an ongoing process that requires foundational work and continuous improvement. Just as a building needs a solid foundation to stand strong, confronting bias starts with fostering self-awareness and creating a safe, inclusive environment. Encouraging perspective taking and implementing accountability measures help organizations adapt and grow stronger. This approach emphasizes that mitigating bias isn't a one-time fix but a perpetual journey, much like the maintenance and strengthening of a building over time to ensure its longevity and safety for all occupants.

To help you reflect on the learning in this chapter and set action items, complete the "Designing Your Blueprint: Addressing Implicit Bias in Schools" reproducible (page 118).

Designing Your Blueprint: Addressing Implicit Bias in Schools

Take some time on your own, in a small group, or during a professional meeting or development opportunity to reflect on, discuss, and examine your own implicit biases and the implications within the classroom and school.

REFLECTION POINTS	TAKE ACTION!
What are some biases you can acknowledge within yourself that you might need to examine and explore within the educational setting?	
In what ways do you actively practice anti-bias leadership in your educational setting (school or classroom)? Can you provide one or two specific examples of policies, practices, or initiatives that demonstrate this?	
How do you address and handle instances of bias when they occur in your school? What measures are in place to ensure a fair and unbiased resolution?	
How do you foster an environment of inclusivity and diversity in your school? How do you ensure that all voices are heard and respected, and every student feels a sense of belonging?	
Name an activity or initiative from this chapter that you could adapt or incorporate into your practice as an educator or education leader.	

A Blueprint for Belonging © 2024 Solution Tree Press • SolutionTree.com
Visit **go.SolutionTree.com/SEL** to download this free reproducible.

CHAPTER 4

RESTORATIVE JUSTICE: REPAIRING HARM AND BUILDING RELATIONSHIPS

Restorative justice is not about forgetting the harm, it's about remembering the humanity of both the victim and the offender.

–Daniel Reisel

It was a frigid morning when Ms. Chen, the principal of Lincoln High School, was confronted with a circumstance that shifted her discipline practices forever. Lincoln High School was situated in a low-income area, where violence and poverty were common. Jason was a quiet, reserved student who always kept to himself. He did his best to take care of his younger siblings while his mom worked multiple jobs just to make ends meet.

Jason's mom struggled with addiction, and his dad had been in and out of prison for most of his life. The family lived in a small, run-down apartment in a dangerous part of town where gang violence was common. He was constantly worried about where his next meal would come from and often went to bed hungry. Jason had always been ashamed of his family's situation and tried to hide it from his classmates and teacher.

For Jason, this particular week had been worse than ever. He hadn't seen his mom for several nights, and bread and mustard were all he could find for his brothers' and sisters' lunches that morning. As soon as he sat down in mathematics class, his classmate Eric began bragging about yet another brand new, expensive hoodie his dad had just bought him. After the bell rang, Jason saw Eric stuff the sweatshirt into his locker, watched as he snapped the lock shut, and waited until Eric was out of sight. Carefully, Jason spun the same numbers he'd seen Eric use to open the lock, pulled out the sweatshirt, and pushed it to the bottom of his bag. Immediately, he heard her voice.

"Stop right there, young man," Ms. Chen exclaimed, as he spun around to see his school's principal standing behind him with arms crossed firmly across her chest.

Normally, intentional theft such as this would have led her to immediately suspend or even expel Jason, but Ms. Chen chose a different path. She had been learning a lot about bias and restorative justice. She knew in her heart that Jason was a "good kid" and that he was dealing with some rough circumstances. Ms. Chen was determined to show him another way to solve his problems. Creating a safe environment where students could thrive was important to her.

She invited Jason and Eric to a restorative justice meeting, hoping to help them reconcile and find a way forward. First, though, she talked to Jason privately, asking him to explain his perspective and feelings, and they explored what might have motivated the theft. For Jason, it was challenging at first to be vulnerable about his feelings and needs. However, he felt like someone finally cared about him and his struggles. Jason shared his struggles with poverty, explaining that he had been envious of Eric, and he had wrongly stolen the sweatshirt to pawn it to buy some groceries for his family.

It was the first time he had revealed his home life to someone at school. Ms. Chen explored some possible solutions with him, including accessing family support services and the local food bank, and made plans to involve child protective services. Then, when he was ready, she invited Eric to join them in her office.

Ms. Chen guided the boys in exploring the situation by stating their observations about the situation, naming their respective feelings, and encouraging them both to identify and state their needs. After learning that his sweatshirt had been stolen, Eric had initially been enraged, but after hearing Jason describe some of his circumstances at home, his frustration turned to empathy. Jason showed accountability for stealing and offered a genuine apology. Moving forward, Jason promised not to steal again and offered to find a new lock for Eric's locker. Eric accepted the apology with grace.

The experience changed Jason's life. He began to see that he was not alone and there were people who cared about him. He started visiting the food bank regularly and then began to volunteer there on weekends. He found a sense of purpose and belonging in serving others in his community. Jason's story inspired Eric, who also began volunteering on Saturdays at the food bank. They were able to look beyond their own differences and offer help to those in need. Eventually, they started an equity club together at their high school, which enabled them to launch an annual fundraiser and food drive for the food bank.

The shift toward restorative justice at Lincoln High School is an example of the significant move from a punitive disciplinary approach to a foundational culture of restoration and accountability.

In this chapter, you will learn how to build on these restorative principles, laying the groundwork for a powerful restorative justice through helpful strategies, addressing the shift from traditional discipline, deconstructing the school-to-prison pipeline, and bolstering essential communication strategies. You also will uncover and address some of the challenges around restorative practices and solutions that can help resolve them. Finally, educators and leaders will find toolbox strategies to design a blueprint where all members of the school environment are responsible for the school culture and sense of belonging.

The Meaning of Restorative Justice

Restorative justice is a powerful tool for repairing harm and building relationships in the school environment. It focuses on restoring relationships rather than punishing offenders, and it allows students to take ownership of their actions and repair harm done to others (Zehr, 2015). Schools can also use restorative justice as a preventive measure, encouraging students to take responsibility for their actions and build stronger relationships with their peers and teachers (Pavelka, 2013).

Restorative justice is a practice that focuses on repairing harm caused by wrongdoing and restoring relationships between the parties involved (Zehr, 2015). Instead of punishment and retribution, restorative justice aims to facilitate dialogue, understanding, and healing, with the goal of building stronger and more compassionate communities. Research shows that restorative justice practices can have positive outcomes for both the individuals affected and the broader community (González & Buth, 2019; Gumz & Grant, 2009). In schools, restorative justice practices can reduce disciplinary referrals and suspensions, increase students' sense of safety and belonging, and improve academic outcomes (Gregory, Clawson, Davis, & Gerewitz, 2016; Payne & Welch, 2015).

Beyond addressing harm, restorative justice practices also involve proactive measures to build a supportive and inclusive community. Researchers Berit Follestad and Nina Wroldsen (2019) state, "Good psychosocial learning environments can strengthen students' sense of belonging to the school community and in doing so can be crucial to prevent negative behavior" (p. 16). Moreover, as our world moves to acknowledge the history of colonization, restorative justice approaches reflect and mirror many Indigenous ways of learning and interacting, offering a more inclusive and culturally sensitive approach to discipline and problem solving within schools (Follestad & Wroldsen, 2019).

As Brown (2018) notes, restorative justice requires a willingness to be vulnerable, listen with empathy, and engage in honest and open dialogue. It requires a shift away from a focus on blame and punishment and toward accountability and healing. By practicing restorative justice, you can create more just and compassionate communities that are better equipped to address conflict and harm in a constructive and transformative manner.

Activities such as community-building circles, where students and teachers regularly gather to share their thoughts and feelings, help foster mutual respect and understanding. These practices help students feel more connected to their peers and teachers, leading to a healthier and more engaging learning environment. As Follestad and Wroldsen (2019) assert, "To participate in a circle gives a sense of belonging. . . . To meet and communicate in a circle increases the possibility for positive safe relationships and a psychosocial atmosphere best described as a collective attention—a sense of 'we'" (p. 22).

Used both proactively and reactively, restorative circles encourage open dialogue and relationship building, and address misbehavior in a more inclusive way than traditional disciplinary actions. When led by peers, students tend to communicate more openly and honestly. The goal is open communication to repair harm and focus on actionable points for future improvement. (The Classroom Toolbox [page 131] and School Leadership Toolbox [page 142] sections provide several different templates, approaches, and frameworks for restorative practices within classrooms and the broader school environment.)

In the following sections, you will explore the principles of restorative practices, how they compare to traditional disciplinary methods, and how you can implement them in your classrooms and schools.

Core Principles of Restorative Justice

Restorative justice practices focus on several guiding principles that underpin their approach (Woolford & Nelund, 2019). The core principles of restorative practices include accountability, empathy, respect, open communication, and community participation (Pavelka, 2013). By understanding these principles, educators and education leaders can better apply restorative justice practices in their schools.

- **Accountability:** Restorative practices require individuals to accept responsibility for their actions. It's not about assigning blame but instead acknowledging one's role in an incident. For example, if a student disrupts class, rather than simply punishing the student, use a restorative approach that requires the student to recognize how their behavior impacted the class and take steps to make amends, such as apologizing to classmates or helping the teacher with a task (Woolford & Nelund, 2019).

- **Empathy:** Understanding and sharing the feelings of others is a critical component of restorative practices. It helps individuals involved in a conflict see the impact of their actions on others. For example, a student who repeatedly talks over others in class might participate in a restorative circle where classmates express how this behavior makes them feel unheard or disrespected (Follestad & Wroldsen, 2019).

- **Respect:** Everyone involved in a restorative justice process is treated with dignity. This respect extends to the way individuals communicate with each other, and how they acknowledge and value different perspectives (Follestad & Wroldsen, 2019). In a restorative conference following a bullying incident, for example, all participants—the bullied student, the bully, witnesses, and facilitators—are treated with equal respect and receive an equal opportunity to voice their feelings and thoughts.

- **Open communication:** Restorative practices thrive on transparency and honesty. This means encouraging open dialogue about incidents and feelings, even when it's uncomfortable (Follestad & Wroldsen, 2019). For example, a teacher who perceives a student as constantly disruptive might engage in an open conversation with them to understand the reasons behind the behavior, which could reveal unseen issues such as learning difficulties or problems at home.

- **Community participation:** Restorative practices recognize that harm affects not just individuals, but the wider community. Including all affected parties in the process of addressing an issue allows for comprehensive healing and resolution (Follestad & Wroldsen, 2019). For example, after a vandalism incident at a school, a restorative meeting might include students, teachers, parents, and even custodial staff who had to clean up, discussing the incident's impact and the path forward.

These core principles provide the foundation for implementing restorative justice practices (Pavelka, 2013). By keeping these principles at the forefront, schools can create a more inclusive, respectful, and supportive learning environment. While these core principles lay a solid groundwork for nurturing an environment of mutual respect and understanding, it is equally important to recognize how they contrast with traditional disciplinary approaches. Transitioning from a paradigm of punitive measures to one of restorative justice requires a shift in perspective: from one that often isolates and punishes to one that seeks to understand, heal, and reintegrate.

Restorative Justice Versus Traditional Discipline

The following scenario offers a comparative analysis of restorative practices and traditional punitive disciplinary approaches, outlining the benefits and potential challenges of each. Understanding the differences between restorative practices and traditional discipline can provide crucial insight into the value of these practices for building healthy school communities.

Alex attends Gaviota Middle School in his small community. His parents are often away on business, and his brother, Owen, plays in a local metal band and is never around. Alex struggles with friendships. Bored, Alex often vandalizes school property on the weekends and evenings by spray-painting graffiti on the school walls. In a traditional disciplinary approach, the school's response might be to suspend Alex. School administrators typically make this decision without involving others affected by the incident.

While this punishment might deter Alex from repeating the action due to fear of further suspensions, it does not necessarily help Alex understand why the action was wrong or how it impacted others. Alex may return to school after the suspension without having made amends or learning how to behave differently in the future.

However, the school-based inclusion team, principal, and Alex's teacher decide to take a restorative approach to the incidents. They invite Alex, his parents, and the custodian to participate in a restorative process to address the harm caused by the graffiti to reinforce accountability and behavioral change.

During this meeting, the custodian expresses how the graffiti creates extra work for him and how his caseload is already stretched to max capacity. He explains that the vandalism takes away from the precious time he has with his sons in the evenings and on the weekends because he is often called out to do overtime work scrubbing the paint off the school or repainting damaged surfaces. Alex's teacher explains how the incidents disrupt the learning environment by causing distraction and how they have to close down certain parts of the school when it needs to be repainted.

Hearing these perspectives, Alex gains an understanding of the real impact of the vandalism—something that a simple suspension might not achieve. As part of the restorative justice process, Alex participates in deciding how to make amends. With suggestions from his parents and school staff, he commits to cleaning the graffiti and offers to offset some of the costs incurred by the school by agreeing to help the custodial staff with the school grounds twice a week for the remainder of the year.

In this restorative scenario, Alex has a chance to learn from his mistakes and take steps to repair the harm done. This can lead to a more meaningful, lasting behavior change than traditional punitive measures. It also helps build understanding and empathy, contributing to a more supportive and respectful school community.

By comparing these two approaches, it's easy to see how restorative practices offer an effective and empathetic alternative to traditional discipline, fostering accountability, learning, and community healing. The next section discusses the school-to-prison pipeline, a systemic issue where punitive measures in educational settings may inadvertently set students on a path toward incarceration rather than rehabilitation.

The School-to-Prison Pipeline and Restorative Justice

The school-to-prison pipeline is a societal trend in which punitive disciplinary measures in schools, often used disproportionately on historically marginalized students, lead to higher rates of suspensions, expulsions, and eventually involvement in the criminal justice system (Sullivan, 2018). This process begins when a student is removed from regular schooling due to disciplinary action. These actions can range from minor infractions, such as tardiness or dress code violations, to more serious behavioral problems (Marder & Kurz, 2023). Students involved in these activities are then typically placed in alternative schools, juvenile detention centers, or other disciplinary programs.

According to Kerrin Wolf and Aaron Kupchik (2017), students who are expelled or suspended are significantly more likely to drop out of school and then become involved in the criminal justice system, and they are more likely to be arrested in adulthood. In the article, "Becoming a Citizen: Habits of National Belonging in the United States," Shannon Sullivan (2018) writes about the school-to-prison pipeline.

> [It] typically operates more subtly, ostracizing, punishing, and leading to the pushing-out of students of color from school, either through suspension, expulsion, or children's dropping out. Once they are pushed out of the educational system, it becomes easy for children of color to find themselves in juvenile detention systems, with formal barriers to re-entry into traditional schools. (p. 170)

The pipeline is perpetuated by zero-tolerance policies, which became more common in schools in the 1990s, intended to crack down on school violence and disruptive behavior. However, these policies often lead to extreme disciplinary measures for minor infractions (Marder & Kurz, 2023). For example, a student could be suspended for a dress code violation or for being tardy. The school-to-prison pipeline is characterized by significant disparities between advantaged and disadvantaged groups. According to the U.S. Department of Education (2016), African American students are 3.8 times more likely to receive one or more out-of-school suspensions as compared to White students.

Similarly, students with disabilities are more than twice as likely to receive an out-of-school suspension than students without disabilities. Additionally, schools in low-income areas often lack resources and support systems to address behavioral issues appropriately, leading to a higher reliance on disciplinary measures (Marder & Kurz, 2023). The introduction of law enforcement officers in schools, often in response to concerns about safety, has also been linked to an increase in school-based arrests, further feeding into the pipeline.

The school-to-prison pipeline is a complex issue involving educational policies, social and economic factors, and systemic racial disparities. Addressing this issue requires comprehensive reform, with a focus on creating equitable, supportive school environments that prioritize education and growth over punitive discipline (Marder & Kurz, 2023).

Restorative justice practices, which focus on building relationships and understanding, can play a key role in this reform. These practices can help dismantle the pipeline by shifting the focus from punishment to healing and understanding, thereby reducing the alienation that can result from traditional punitive methods

(Marder & Kurz, 2023). It promotes community and relationship building, reduces suspensions and expulsions by addressing issues at their root, and cultivates key social-emotional skills. Restorative justice can help address the racial and socioeconomic disparities inherent in traditional school discipline, promoting a more equitable environment. Thus, restorative justice can serve as a powerful alternative to traditional discipline methods, contributing significantly to the dismantling of the school-to-prison pipeline.

Communication and Restorative Justice

Respectful communication is the cornerstone of restorative justice in schools, providing a structured approach to resolving conflicts and building relationships. Follestad and Wroldsen (2019) delineate four critical steps in effective communication.

1. **Observation:** Begin by neutrally describing a specific action or behavior; for example: "During group work, you spoke loudly and interrupted your classmates."

2. **Feeling:** Communicate the emotions that the behavior elicited; for example: "This made me feel concerned."

3. **Need:** Articulate the underlying needs linked to these feelings; for example: "I need a classroom where everyone feels heard and respected."

4. **Request:** Make a clear and actionable request to meet the identified needs; for example: "Please lower your voice and allow others to finish speaking before you contribute."

In practice, this approach empowers educators to address student behaviors with empathy, fostering an environment where every student's voice is heard and valued. Similarly, Jennifer Abrams (2009) and Kim Scott (2017) advocate for open dialogue and mutual respect to cultivate a positive and accountable school culture. Building on this foundation, six essential elements underpin respectful communication.

1. **Build relationships:** Form trust-based relationships within the school community, showing genuine care for everyone's experiences and challenges. This involves getting to know students and staff on a personal level, understanding their challenges and aspirations, and showing genuine interest and care for their well-being. After all, we all spend so much time together in the school setting that starting it off right is essential!

2. **Create a safe space:** Foster an environment conducive to open conversations, with privacy and comfort for honest expression. This means setting aside time for one-on-one meetings, ensuring privacy, and creating

an atmosphere where everyone feels comfortable and safe to express their thoughts (Abrams, 2009; Scott, 2017).

3. **Practice radical candor:** Combine direct feedback with empathy, articulating care in difficult conversations. This involves challenging directly while also caring personally (Scott, 2017). Provide clear, direct feedback, but do it in a way that communicates empathy and understanding.

4. **Use "I" statements:** Maintain respect and empathy by focusing on personal feelings and perspectives, avoiding blame. Use "I" statements to express your feelings and perspectives and listen attentively to the other person's perspective (Abrams, 2009).

5. **Find common ground and solutions:** Collaboratively seek solutions, respecting and validating differing viewpoints. This involves understanding the other person's viewpoint, validating their feelings, and working together to address the issue at hand (Abrams, 2009; Scott, 2017).

6. **Follow up:** Ensure the implementation of solutions through consistent follow-up and check-ins. This could involve scheduling a follow-up meeting or periodically checking in to see how things are progressing (Scott, 2017).

Respectful communication through these methods addresses immediate issues and strengthens the fabric of the school community, laying the groundwork for effective restorative practices and a supportive learning environment.

Obstacles to Restorative Justice Practices

Implementing restorative practices in schools, like any substantial change, can come with challenges and obstacles. Understanding these obstacles and developing strategies to address them can help ensure a successful transition to a restorative approach (Marder & Kurz, 2023; Woolford & Nelund, 2019). The following are some obstacles a school might face in implementing restorative justice practices.

- **Resistance to change:** Some staff members or parents might be resistant to the shift from traditional disciplinary methods to restorative practices. They may believe in the effectiveness of traditional punishments, or they may feel that restorative practices are too lenient. You might address resistance by engaging these stakeholders in dialogue about the benefits and philosophy of restorative practices, and by providing

Restorative Justice: Repairing Harm and Building Relationships

success stories and research supporting their effectiveness (Follestad & Wroldsen, 2019).

- **Lack of training:** Staff might lack the necessary skills or knowledge to implement restorative practices effectively (Follestad & Wroldsen, 2019). Professional development workshops can be beneficial, focusing on the principles of restorative practices, communication skills, facilitating restorative circles, and dealing with challenging situations.

- **Time constraints:** Restorative practices can be time consuming. Organizing a restorative circle or conference requires more time than assigning detention (Marder & Kurz, 2023). However, it's important to remember that these practices often address issues at their roots, potentially saving time in the long run by reducing recurring conflicts (Follestad & Wroldsen, 2019).

- **Inadequate resources:** Schools might lack the necessary resources, such as dedicated staff or physical spaces, to implement restorative practices (Marder & Kurz, 2023). Creating partnerships with community organizations or seeking grant opportunities can be potential solutions. Refer to the activity Diversity and Inclusion Partnerships With Community Organizations (page 102), and use some of these partnerships to explore securing potential external resources.

- **Misunderstanding of the approach:** Stakeholders might misunderstand restorative practices as an approach that allows misbehavior to go unpunished (Marder & Kurz, 2023). Communication and education can clear this misconception, emphasizing that restorative practices are about accountability and learning rather than simply punishing or ignoring inappropriate behavior.

- **Initial increase in reported incidents:** As restorative practices encourage open communication, schools may see an initial rise in the number of reported incidents (Marder & Kurz, 2023). Some might misinterpret this as an increase in conflicts, but it's often a sign that students feel more comfortable bringing issues to light.

To overcome these obstacles, it is vital to provide thorough training, encourage open dialogue, ensure adequate resources, and highlight the long-term benefits of restorative practices (Woolford & Nelund, 2019). It may also be helpful to implement restorative practices gradually, starting with a pilot program or implementing them in stages, so the school community can learn and adjust along the way.

Evaluation and Continuous Improvement of Restorative Justice Practices

It is important to acknowledge the value of ongoing evaluation and adjustment of restorative practices to meet the changing needs of students and the school community (Woolford & Nelund, 2019). Embracing the dynamic and ever-changing nature of educational settings, it's crucial to acknowledge the necessity of ongoing evaluation and adaptation of restorative practices (Pavelka, 2013). This continual assessment provides an opportunity to stay responsive to the evolving needs of students and the wider school community.

To ensure the effectiveness of restorative practices, educators should make data-driven decisions based on key indicators like the frequency of incidents, types of conflicts, and student feedback. This evaluation should not only focus on problem areas but also identify successful practices that lead to positive outcomes, fostering a culture of learning from both challenges and successes.

Moreover, as students grow and the school environment changes, adjust and refine restorative practices to meet these new circumstances. By keeping a pulse on the changing dynamics, you can tailor strategies to students' needs, fostering a climate that is not only reactive to challenges, but also proactive in creating a harmonious school community.

In essence, the journey toward a restorative approach to discipline is a continuous process of learning, evaluating, and adapting (Pavelka, 2013). This cyclical process ensures that methods stay relevant, effective, and firmly centered on the well-being of all members of the school community.

The following Classroom Toolbox and School Leadership Toolbox sections strive to equip educators and school leaders with the understanding and tools needed to foster a more compassionate, effective, and inclusive approach to discipline.

CLASSROOM TOOLBOX

> By focusing on the BUILD elements—boundaries, understanding, integrity, listening, and dependability—teachers can use these activities to promote and implement restorative justice practices in their classroom.

Mindfulness Practices

🤝 Integrity

Mindfulness practices can help students develop self-awareness, self-regulation, and empathy (Michael, 2022). Start with an introduction to explain the benefits of mindfulness and set expectations. Next, guide students through a mindfulness meditation. Then, give students time to reflect on their experience. Finally, discuss ways students can apply mindfulness in their daily lives.

The following is an example of a mindfulness meditation for students ages 9–12 with a restorative justice purpose (Michael, 2022).

1. **Introduction:** Begin by asking students to find a comfortable seated position with their feet on the ground and their hands resting on their knees. Invite them to close their eyes or soften their gaze and take a few deep breaths.

2. **Body scan:** Guide students through a body scan, starting at the top of the head and slowly working down to the toes. Encourage them to notice any areas of tension or discomfort and simply observe those sensations without judgment. Noticing how your body reacts to stress or tension is an important step in self-awareness.

3. **Gratitude practice:** Ask students to recall someone or something they feel grateful for. Encourage them to picture this person or thing in their mind and take a moment to fully appreciate the positive impact it has had on their life.

4. **Forgiveness practice:** Next, invite students to think of someone with whom they have had a conflict or who has hurt them in some way. Ask them to picture this person in their mind and repeat the following phrases silently to themselves: "I forgive you for any harm you have caused me, whether intentional or unintentional. I release any anger or resentment I may be holding toward you, and I wish you peace and happiness."

Encourage students to repeat these phrases as many times as needed to feel a sense of release and forgiveness.

5. **Compassion practice:** Ask students to recall someone who may be struggling or suffering in some way. Encourage them to picture this person in their mind and repeat the following phrases silently to themselves: "May you be happy. May you be healthy. May you be safe. May you live with ease." Encourage students to repeat these phrases several times and to send feelings of compassion and kindness toward this person.

6. **Conclusion:** End the meditation by inviting students to take a few deep breaths and slowly open their eyes. Encourage them to carry the feelings of gratitude, forgiveness, and compassion with them throughout the day.

Community Connection Circles

Understanding, Listening

Choose a time for regular circles and set a topic or question for discussion, similar to the way you would establish a morning meeting (see chapter 2, page 39; Follestad & Wroldsen, 2019). To bolster the activity, have an anonymous ask-it basket, wonder box, or ponder pod in your classroom that students access anonymously to pose questions, suggest topics, or raise concerns. Screen students' questions before addressing them within the whole-group setting.

1. Arrange classroom seating in a circle to encourage equality and openness.

2. Establish and refer to ground rules for respectful listening and speaking.

3. Facilitate the circle, allowing each student to speak in turn without interruption (Follestad & Wroldsen, 2019).

4. Start with a check-in, offering students an opportunity to share something about themselves, moving around the circle in a clockwise direction. Sometimes using a talking object (for example, feather, stone, or stick) can serve as a visual reminder not to interrupt when others are speaking.

5. Build in lightheartedness through a game or icebreaker activity (Follestad & Wroldsen, 2019). The following are twenty-five of my favorite icebreakers and morale boosters for classroom and staff meetings. These activities are designed to foster connection, teamwork, and communication among students of all ages. Each activity serves a unique purpose in building community, enhancing social skills, or simply breaking the ice in a fun and engaging way.

- **Bingo icebreaker:** Students fill out bingo cards by finding classmates with specific characteristics listed on the card.
- **Blind drawing:** One student describes a picture, and their team tries to draw it without seeing it.
- **Break the code game:** Teams try to decipher a code or solve a riddle using clues.
- **Charades:** Students act out a word or phrase without speaking and teammates guess what it is.
- **Class mural:** Students collaborate on a large-scale art project, contributing to a collective masterpiece.
- **Class talent show:** Students showcase their unique talents in a class talent show.
- **Compliment chain:** Students sit in a circle and take turns complimenting the person to their right.
- **Egg drop challenge:** Teams design a contraption to protect an egg from breaking when dropped from a certain height.
- **Four corners on moral dilemmas:** Each corner of the classroom represents a response, such as "agree," "disagree," "strongly agree," and "strongly disagree." Propose a moral dilemma to students, who then choose a corner based on their stance about that topic or a "would you rather" question. Students can then discuss their opinions and provide evidence in an attempt to convince their peers to agree with them in a debate-type format.
- **Four small words:** Students try to communicate complex ideas using only four simple words.
- **Fruit salad game:** Assign students to fruit names, and then have them sit in a circle. Have them switch seats when their fruit is called. This fast-paced activity promotes quick thinking and physical activity. It can serve as a fun break and a way to learn about different fruits, enhancing both physical and cognitive skills.
- **Group juggling:** Students pass multiple objects around the circle, ensuring everyone catches and throws each object once.
- **High-five train:** Students form two lines and high five each other while sharing positive news.

- **Human knot:** Students hold hands across a circle and try to untangle themselves without releasing hands.
- **Joke day:** Students share their favorite jokes, bringing laughter to the classroom.
- **Paper tower:** Teams compete to build the tallest tower using only paper and tape within a set time.
- **Positive affirmation cards:** Students write positive affirmations on index cards that the teacher provides, each with a different name on them. Students then think of a positive compliment or affirmation about the specific student on their card and then exchange cards with classmates.
- **Positive name game:** Each student assigns a positive adjective to themselves that starts with the same letter as their name. During the morning message, have students "re-introduce" themselves to the class using this positive adjective. The goal is to help students think of positive traits or attributions about themselves.
- **Relay race:** Students participate in a race in which they complete a series of tasks as a team.
- **Scavenger hunt:** Teams race to find a list of items within the classroom (related to a topic of instruction or a set of questions related to experiences they've had) within a set time period. For example, a teacher could adapt the activity to a mathematics lesson on measurement by asking students to find a measuring implement or something that is longer than their pinky finger. A "getting-to-know-you" scavenger hunt requires students to find classmates to sign their sheet of paper if they match a particular description (such as *Find someone who has traveled outside of this state*, or *Find someone whose favorite color is blue*).
- **Secret friend:** Students perform anonymous acts of kindness for an assigned "secret friend" for a week.
- **Silent lineup:** Students line up in order of their birthdays without speaking, using only nonverbal communication.
- **Smile pass:** Students sit in a circle and pass a smile from one person to the next.

- **Texas hug:** Students greet each other with a hearty handshake and a friendly pat on the back, promoting camaraderie.
- **Two truths and a lie:** Students share two true facts and one lie about themselves, while classmates try to guess the lie.

6. Discuss one of the topics or concerns suggested by students in the "ask-it basket" or that has come up as a class through a hands-on activity, demonstration, or discussion. Some topics might include learning to line up respectfully, how to deal with hurt feelings, or how to improve overall communication (Follestad & Wroldsen, 2019).

7. Ask for feedback about the experience, inviting students to reflect on their learning, emotions, and thoughts.

8. Check out with students with a routine or ritualistic activity that signals the community connection circle has ended. For example, students could pass an object around the circle and thank one another. Another option might be to offer an opportunity for a brief reflection of the activity.

9. If there is a problem to be solved, it might be helpful to move on to another strategy, such as Restorative Chats or Peace Corners (page 136).

Restorative Chats

Understanding, Listening

When addressing problem behaviors with students, it's essential to approach the situation with care and respect, aiming to guide them toward self-awareness and positive change. Here's how you can effectively manage such situations through a constructive and empathetic conversation.

1. Identify the problem behavior or incident (for example, the student often interrupts and talks loudly during group discussions).

2. Initiate a one-on-one conversation with the student involved, ensuring a private, nonthreatening environment. For example:

> Teacher: Alexa, can we chat for a moment privately? I've noticed you often talk loudly and interrupt during group discussions. What do you think?
>
> Alexa: I get excited and want to share my ideas.

3. Encourage the student to reflect on their behavior, asking open-ended questions like, "What happened?" and "Who do you think was affected by your actions?"

> Teacher: I appreciate your enthusiasm, but how might this affect others?
>
> Alexa: They might feel annoyed and unheard.
>
> Teacher: Exactly, it can disrupt the learning environment.

4. Facilitate the student in identifying a way to make amends or change behavior in the future.

> Teacher: Let's think of ways to share your ideas without interrupting. What could you do differently?
>
> Alexa: I could raise my hand or wait for others to finish speaking.
>
> Teacher: Great! How about writing down your ideas to share later?
>
> Alexa: I can do that.
>
> Teacher: Thanks, Alexa. Let's try these strategies in the next discussion.

Peace Corners

Understanding, Integrity, Listening

A peace corner is a designated space where students can go to calm down, reflect, and practice self-regulation when they feel overwhelmed or upset. It's equipped with tools and resources to help students manage their emotions and return to the classroom ready to learn (Murphy, 2019). Integrating a peace corner into the classroom environment can significantly contribute to nurturing students' emotional intelligence and self-regulation skills.

Consider the following steps for implementing a peace corner in the classroom.

1. **Start off on the right foot:** Begin by conducting an orientation session for students about the peace corner. Explain that its purpose is to offer a safe space for calming down, reflecting, and regaining control over their emotions before rejoining classroom activities.

2. **Role-play scenarios:** In large-group minilessons, use role play to demonstrate scenarios where using the peace corner would be appropriate. For example, students might use it as a strategy for managing feelings of anger, frustration, or overwhelming sadness.

3. **Establish guidelines and strategies:** Teach students specific self-regulation strategies, such as deep-breathing exercises, mindfulness, or guided imagery, that they can practice in the peace corner. Place visual cues or written prompts in the peace corner to help guide students through calming techniques or reflective practices, like thinking about a peaceful place or writing down how they feel and why. Timers can be an effective way to manage students' time in the peace corner, ensuring it remains available for others and that the time spent there is focused on calming and reflecting.

4. **Offer helpful tools:** Provide stress balls, sensory toys, or fidget spinners that students can use to help manage their stress or anxiety physically. Offer notebooks, coloring books, or drawing materials for students to express their emotions creatively. Writing prompts or coloring can serve as a peaceful distraction and a way of processing feelings. Include simple, age-appropriate mindfulness or meditation guides, possibly through audio recordings or illustrated books, to help students practice mindfulness.

5. **Provide oversight:** While the peace corner should be a student-managed space, teachers should discreetly monitor its use to ensure students are using it appropriately and to identify students who may need additional support.

By providing clear guidelines, specific activities, and ongoing support, the peace corner can become a cornerstone of emotional learning and self-regulation in the classroom. This proactive approach supports individual students in managing their emotions and fosters a classroom environment that values understanding, integrity, and active listening.

The Circle Process

♡ Understanding, 🤝 Integrity, 🔊 Listening

The circle process is a distinctive restorative justice practice aimed at fostering dialogue, building relationships, and addressing harm within educational settings. Unlike morning meetings or community connection circles, which generally focus on setting the tone for the day, discussing daily activities, and enhancing classroom community through structured conversations, the circle process delves deeper into conflict resolution, emotional healing, and communal rebuilding after incidents of harm (Costello, Wachtel, & Wachtel, 2009; Thorsborne & Blood, 2013). The following are steps for implementing the circle process.

1. **Preparation:** Effective facilitation by a teacher or school leader begins with preparation. Educators or administrators trained in restorative justice practices should curate a safe, inclusive environment. This groundwork ensures students and staff feel valued and respected, which is crucial for open dialogue (Morrison, 2007; Zehr, 2015).

2. **Opening:** The session starts with a warm welcome and a clear articulation of the circle's purpose in solving a problem or conflict in the classroom or within the school. Establishing ground rules promotes a respectful, confidential space conducive to honesty and vulnerability (Morrison, 2007).

3. **Check-in:** Participants share personal insights or experiences relevant to the topic or the issue at hand. This step is vital for nurturing connections and emphasizing the community aspect of the circle (Van Ness & Strong, 2014).

4. **Storytelling:** Individuals directly involved in the incident share their narratives, fostering empathy and understanding through active listening. This phase allows all sides to articulate their perspectives and feelings (Zehr, 2015). Possible questions include the following.
    - "Can you tell us what happened from your perspective?"
    - "What were you thinking at the time?"

5. **Dialogue and reflection:** The group engages in a guided discussion, focusing on constructive, respectful dialogue. This facilitates mutual understanding and explores the impact of the harm caused (Van Ness & Strong, 2014). Examples of questions for the person who caused harm include the following.

Restorative Justice: Repairing Harm and Building Relationships 139

- "Who do you think has been affected by what happened?"
- "In what way do you think they have been affected?"
- "Can you describe what impact this experience or incident has had on you?"
- "What has been the hardest part for you?"
- "What do you feel needs to happen to make things right?"

6. **Repair and healing:** Together, participants brainstorm actionable steps toward reconciliation, accountability, and future harm prevention, emphasizing collective responsibility in healing (Morrison, 2007).
    - "How can we ensure this does not happen again?"
    - "What do you think we should do going forward?"
    - "What can we do collectively to repair relationships and rebuild trust?"
    - "What might be a good first step toward making that happen?"

7. **Closing:** The facilitator summarizes key insights and discusses follow-up actions, reinforcing the session's communal spirit and shared commitments (Costello et al., 2009).

The following scenario shows how the circle process can help you address exclusionary behavior.

Three fourth-grade girls, Ava, Bella, and Chloe, often play together during recess. Emily, who is new to the school, has attempted to join them several times but has been consistently left out. One day, when Emily asks if she can play with them on the swings, Bella bluntly tells her, "You're too fat for the swings." Emily is deeply hurt by this comment and withdraws from the group, feeling isolated and shamed.

Preparation: The teacher, Mrs. Martinez, notices Emily's sadness after recess, learning about the behavior of the other girls. She decides to use the circle process to address the issue, hoping to foster understanding and empathy, and repair the harm done. Mrs. Martinez understands the importance of a supportive and nonjudgmental environment.

Opening: Mrs. Martinez gathers Ava, Bella, Chloe, and Emily in a quiet, comfortable space in the classroom during the next recess break. She begins by telling the girls that she wants to discuss a situation that has caused harm and is hoping to work together toward healing and understanding.

Check-in: Mrs. Martinez invites each girl to share how they are feeling without discussing the incident. This helps to establish a communal space where everyone's voice is heard.

Storytelling: Emily shares her experience first. She explains how she feels when she's left out and especially when Bella called her "too fat" to use the swings. She expresses feeling hurt, embarrassed, and unwelcome.

Bella then speaks. She admits to saying those words and acknowledges that she was thoughtless and didn't consider Emily's feelings. Ava and Chloe share that they didn't intervene and recognize their part in making Emily feel excluded.

Dialogue and reflection: Mrs. Martinez facilitates a discussion, asking the girls how they think their actions or inactions affected Emily and what feelings might arise from being excluded and insulted.

Repair and healing: The group brainstorms ways to make amends and prevent similar situations in the future. Bella apologizes sincerely to Emily. They all agree to include Emily in their games and work on being more inclusive and mindful of others' feelings.

Closing: Mrs. Martinez summarizes the key points discussed and the commitments made by each girl. She thanks them for their honesty and willingness to resolve the situation. She suggests that they all create a "kindness promise" that includes being kind and inclusive, which they all agree to sign.

Sample dialogue:

Emily: When I heard Bella say that to me, I felt really bad about myself. It hurt my feelings a lot.

Bella: I'm sorry, Emily. I felt like I wanted to play with Ava and Chloe alone. I didn't think before I spoke. I can see how my words hurt you.

Ava and Chloe: We're sorry too for not speaking up. We don't want to hurt your feelings. We didn't know what to say.

Mrs. Martinez: It's important we learn from this. How can we make sure everyone feels included in the future?

All: We can make sure to invite everyone to play and speak up if we hear hurtful comments.

This scenario provides an example of how you can use the circle process to address common conflicts and promote a more inclusive and understanding school environment. The following are some references that provide further information on the circle process.

- *Circle Forward: Building a Restorative School Community* by Carolyn Boyes-Watson and Kay Pranis (2015)
- *The Little Book of Circle Processes: A New/Old Approach to Peacemaking* by Kay Pranis (2005)
- *Using Restorative Circles in Schools: How to Build Strong Learning Communities and Foster Student Wellbeing* by Berit Follestad and Nina Wroldsen (2019)

SCHOOL LEADERSHIP TOOLBOX

> By focusing on the BUILD elements—boundaries, understanding, integrity, listening, and dependability—school leaders can use these activities to promote and implement restorative justice practices in their school.

Restorative Staff Meetings

♡ Understanding,   🤝 Integrity,   🔊 Listening

Foster a collaborative environment by occasionally holding staff meetings in a community connection circle format. In this setting, each staff member gets an equal opportunity to voice their thoughts, feelings, or concerns about a given topic (Costello et al., 2009). For example, a school facing a bullying issue could hold a staff meeting to discuss and collectively devise proactive strategies. This approach encourages empathy and understanding among the staff, leading to a stronger, more harmonious team (Thorsborne & Blood, 2013).

Restorative staff meetings differ significantly from traditional staff meetings by prioritizing open dialogue, sharing of feelings, equity of voice, and collective problem solving within a framework of mutual respect and understanding. This approach is rooted in restorative justice principles, aiming to strengthen relationships and address issues collaboratively. The following is an example scenario of a restorative staff meeting.

A school is grappling with an increase in bullying incidents. The principal decides to hold a restorative staff meeting to address the issue collectively. The meeting takes place in a circle to promote openness and equality. The principal introduces a talking piece for attendees to pass around to ensure that only the person holding it speaks, allowing for uninterrupted sharing.

Opening: The principal opens the meeting by acknowledging the concern and emphasizing the goal of working together to create a safer, more inclusive school environment. She provides a brief overview of the bullying incidents, emphasizing the need for collective action and support.

Check-in: Each staff member is invited to share how they are currently feeling, or a personal reflection related to the issue of bullying, without going into solutions or criticisms.

Dialogue and reflection: As staff pass around the talking piece, each member shares their observations, experiences with bullying in their area, and potential reasons behind the increase in incidents. This round focuses on understanding the issue from multiple perspectives.

Idea generation: The talking piece circulates again, this time for staff to propose strategies and solutions. Ideas might include implementing peer mediation programs, conducting empathy workshops, or revising the school's bullying policy.

Consensus and action planning: The group discusses the proposed strategies, aiming to reach a consensus on a multifaceted action plan. Staff members divide responsibilities to ensure accountability.

Closing: The principal summarizes the decisions made, thanks everyone for their contributions, and outlines the next steps, including when the group will reconvene to review progress.

By embracing the principles of restorative justice in a staff meeting, teachers, school faculty, and leaders can collectively solve relevant problems in a respectful and equitable manner.

Professional Development

◯ Boundaries,   🤝 Integrity,   🛡 Dependability

Regular professional development workshops on restorative practices are essential for equipping staff with the knowledge and skills they need. Topics could include facilitating community connection circles and conducting restorative chats (Kervick, Moore, Ballysingh, Garnett, & Smith, 2019). Ongoing support and coaching ensure that staff can effectively implement restorative practices in the classroom and beyond (Gregory et al., 2016). To enhance professional development focused on restorative justice within a school staff, consider implementing a multifaceted approach, such as the following.

- **Host interactive workshops:** Conduct hands-on sessions in which staff can practice restorative techniques, like circle facilitations and conflict resolution strategies.

- **Invite restorative justice experts to school:** Bring in practitioners with real-world experience to share insights and practical advice.

- **Facilitate peer learning:** Create opportunities for staff to share their experiences and learn from each other through peer-led discussions and reflections.

- **Incorporate simulation exercises:** Use role playing to deepen understanding of different perspectives within restorative processes. Use examples from teachers and current issues bubbling up in your school.

- **Offer ongoing support:** Provide continuous coaching and access to online resources for staff to refine their skills over time. Peer-to-peer coaching can be important for accountability measures too.

- **Engage in reflective practices:** Regularly schedule sessions for staff to reflect on their application of restorative practices, encouraging growth and adaptation. Asking what's working and what's not working are good ways to identify wins (successes) and growth (stretches).

By adopting these strategies, schools and districts can build a robust professional development program that empowers educators to effectively implement restorative justice practices.

Parent and Community Engagement

⊘ Boundaries,   🤝 Integrity,   ☑ Dependability

Engaging parents and community members is crucial for the success of restorative practices. Organize information sessions or workshops to introduce these concepts, and invite feedback and concerns (McCluskey et al., 2008). Involving parents and community members in restorative practices, such as participating in restorative conferences, can foster a stronger, more supportive school community (Morrison, 2007). To foster great communication with parents around restorative practices, focus on three key strategies to make the process more engaging and effective.

1. **Keep it conversational:** Host casual coffee chats or informal meetings where parents can freely ask questions and share their thoughts on restorative practices. This means creating a welcoming atmosphere where dialogue flows easily, much like a friendly chat over coffee.

2. **Employ interactive learning:** Invite parents to hands-on workshop evenings where they can actively participate in learning about restorative practices. This approach makes the learning process fun and engaging, ensuring parents leave with a clear, practical understanding of the concept.

3. **Share successes:** Highlight and share stories of positive outcomes from restorative practices within the school community. Whether through newsletters, social media, or community meetings, showcasing real-life success stories can inspire and build trust among parents.

By making communication conversational, interactive, and positive, you can build stronger, more open relationships with parents, encouraging their active support and participation in restorative practices.

Cultivating Creative Tension

◯ Boundaries,   🤝 Integrity,   🛡 Dependability

Cultivating creative tension is a dynamic strategy aimed at fostering innovation and growth within teams or organizations (Smith & Lewis, 2022). It depends on the delicate balance between maintaining a safe, respectful environment and encouraging the exploration of diverse, even conflicting, ideas. With this approach, disagreement and divergent thinking, when managed constructively, can lead to breakthroughs and creative solutions. The following are some strategies for cultivating creative tension.

- **Establish clear boundaries:** Define what respectful and constructive disagreement looks like within your team. It's crucial to set ground rules that promote open dialogue but prohibit personal attacks, ensuring a focus on ideas rather than individuals.

- **Foster an atmosphere of trust:** Cultivating an environment where team members feel safe to express divergent views without fear of retribution is essential. Trust encourages risk taking and honest feedback, which are key components of creative tension.

- **Encourage divergent thinking:** Stimulate creativity by inviting team members to challenge the status quo and explore unconventional solutions. Workshops, brainstorming sessions, and creative prompts can help unlock new perspectives.

- **Leverage conflicting perspectives:** Actively seek out and incorporate different viewpoints. This can be facilitated through structured debates or role-playing scenarios, or by inviting external experts to challenge internal assumptions.

- **Encourage iteration:** Encourage experimentation through quickly generating and trying new ideas. Create systems where these prototypes can be critiqued and refined, allowing the best ideas to be honed and improved.

Creating this kind of creative tension is about pushing the boundaries of comfort to spark innovation, while ensuring integrity and dependability in how these processes are managed.

Conclusion

This chapter introduced restorative practices as essential tools for creating a supportive learning environment, moving away from punitive measures to focus on healing, learning, and building community. Restorative practices are pivotal in fostering belonging by repairing and strengthening relationships within the school community. They aim to address misbehavior but also mend the harm done to relationships and the community, ensuring every member feels valued and included.

To address potential challenges, such as resistance from staff or parents and the need for resources and training, this chapter offered strategies such as comprehensive training and step-by-step implementation. To keep pace with the changing needs of students and the school community, it's crucial to regularly revisit and refine these practices, ensuring they remain effective and responsive. This approach lays a solid foundation for a more inclusive, understanding, and connected school environment.

To help you reflect on the learning in this chapter and determine action items, complete the "Designing Your Blueprint: Restorative Justice and Building Relationships" reproducible.

Designing Your Blueprint: Restorative Justice and Building Relationships

Take some time on your own, in a small group, or during a professional meeting or development opportunity to explore some of the ways restorative justice can support inclusive, peaceful, and cooperative cultures of belonging and understanding.

REFLECTION POINTS	TAKE ACTION!
How can restorative practices shift the existing disciplinary culture in your school, and what steps can you take to initiate this transformation?	
How can you use restorative practices to strengthen relationships not just among students, but also between students and staff, fostering a greater sense of community and belonging?	
What specific steps can you take to include more voices in your restorative practices, particularly those who may feel marginalized or excluded?	
What is one practice from this chapter that you can implement this week, month, or year to reinforce restorative justice within your school community?	

A Blueprint for Belonging © 2024 Solution Tree Press • SolutionTree.com
Visit **go.SolutionTree.com/SEL** to download this free reproducible.

EPILOGUE

As educators continue to navigate the ongoing challenges of creating a cohesive, collaborative, and restorative school environment, it has become even more evident that a sense of belonging is critical for students' academic success, social-emotional development, and overall well-being. This book is a practical guide for educators and school leaders committed to fostering a culture of belonging in their school community. It examined the latest research and practical examples to provide strategies for creating a positive and inclusive educational environment.

In each chapter, you explored different aspects of belonging, from the foundational elements of self-leadership, to fostering cultures of kindness and generosity, examining implicit biases, and exploring restorative justice practices, providing a road map for building a positive school culture from the ground up. This road map can help you prioritize belonging in your school and provide a more positive, supportive, and inclusive educational environment that benefits everyone involved.

As you reflect on this journey, remember the importance of the building blocks that compose schools and classrooms. The metaphor of constructing a building has woven its way throughout your exploration, serving as a steadfast reminder of the persistent work and committed hearts required to cultivate cultures of belonging in your school.

Like an architect, you can sketch blueprints for inclusive and equitable school communities, detailing the unique contours of what it means to belong. The cornerstone of this architectural marvel we, as educators, strive for is the BUILD framework—boundaries, understanding, integrity, listening, and dependability. These are not just academic concepts, but rather scaffolding that gives rise to a culture of belonging that embraces the beautiful diversity that each member brings to the educational edifice.

In an educational landscape that is dynamic and often challenging, the steadfast strength of clear and compassionate boundaries provides the groundwork on which we stand as educators. Understanding is an essential pillar that supports the edifice, allowing you to honor and cherish the rich tapestry of identities, cultures, and experiences within your school community.

It's not enough to construct beautiful exteriors; your commitment to inclusion and equity must be the rebar within your concrete, providing a resilient internal structure to your school. It requires courage to shine a light on the areas where you can improve, acknowledging biases and taking actionable steps toward rectification.

The stories I shared, from the transformative leadership of Sara Martinez to the inspiring initiatives at schools across North America, are testaments to the power of listening. They reinforce that genuine, empathetic listening is not simply a passive act but a dynamic process that can bring about profound change in our schools and communities.

Finally, through this journey, you've realized that dependability is the capstone of the BUILD framework. Like the roof that shields a building, dependability protects and strengthens your commitments to inclusion and equity, keeping your efforts consistent and reliable.

Our collective journey as educators to build cultures of belonging doesn't end with the closing of this book. In fact, it's a continuous and evolving process, much like constructing a structure that withstands the test of time. As architects of belonging, we have an immense responsibility and a tremendous opportunity to shape not just the buildings, but the lives that dwell within them.

So, I invite you to take up your tools—your compassion, your patience, your expertise—and continue to construct communities of belonging. You have the power to BUILD schools where every student is seen, heard, and valued, where every student—regardless of race, gender, religion, ability, or any other factor—feels a sense of belonging.

Together, we can create a school community that is as strong and as welcoming as a well-built home. In doing so, we contribute to a better, more inclusive future for our students, and indeed for all of us. Because in the end, belonging isn't just about building better schools; it's about building a better world. Here's to our shared commitment in creating this reality, one brick, one story, one student at a time.

REFERENCES AND RESOURCES

Abrams, J. (2009). *Having hard conversations.* Thousand Oaks, CA: Corwin.

Afsar, B., & Umrani, W. A. (2020). Transformational leadership and innovative work behavior: The role of motivation to learn, task complexity and innovation climate. *European Journal of Innovation Management, 23*(3), 402–428. https://doi.org/10.1108/EJIM-12-2018-0257

Aguilar, E. (2018). *Onward: Cultivating emotional resilience in educators.* San Francisco: Jossey-Bass.

Allen, K.-A., Kern, M. L., Vella-Brodrick, D., Hattie, J., & Waters, L. (2018). What schools need to know about fostering school belonging: A meta-analysis. *Educational Psychology Review, 30*(1), 1–34. Accessed at www.researchgate.net/publication/309224583_What_Schools_Need_to_Know_About_Fostering_School_Belonging_a_Meta-analysis on March 19, 2024.

Allen, K.-A., Waters, L., Arslan, G., & Prentice, M. (2022). Strength-based parenting and stress-related growth in adolescents: Exploring the role of positive reappraisal, school belonging, and emotional processing during the pandemic. *Journal of Adolescence, 94*(2), 176–190. https://doi.org/10.1002/jad.12016

Allen, T. J., & Henn, G. (2007). *The organization and architecture of innovation: Managing the flow of technology.* Oxford, UK: Butterworth-Heinemann.

American Psychological Association. (n.d.). *Improving students' relationships with teachers to provide essential supports for learning.* Accessed at www.apa.org/education-career/k12/relationships on November 6, 2023.

Anxiety and Depression Association of America. (2022, October 28). *Anxiety disorders—Facts & statistics.* Accessed at https://adaa.org/understanding-anxiety/facts-statistics on November 6, 2023.

Baldassar, L., Nedelcu, M., Merla, L., & Wilding, R. (2016). ICT-based co-presence in transnational families and communities: Challenging the premise of face-to-face proximity in sustaining relationships. *Global Networks, 16*(2), 133–144. https://doi.org/10.1111/glob.12108

Banaji, M. R., & Greenwald, A. G. (2013). *Blindspot: Hidden biases of good people*. New York: Delacorte Press.

Barzun, M. (2021). *The power of giving away power: How the best leaders learn to let go*. New York: Optimism Press.

Basham, J. D., Blackorby, J., & Marino, M. T. (2020). Opportunity in crisis: The role of Universal Design for Learning in educational redesign. *Learning Disabilities: A Contemporary Journal*, *18*(1), 71–91. Accessed at https://eric.ed.gov/?id=EJ1264277 on March 19, 2024.

Baumeister, R. F., & Leary, M. R. (1995). The need to belong: Desire for interpersonal attachments as a fundamental human motivation. *Psychological Bulletin*, *117*(3), 497–529.

Berger, R., Rugen, L., & Woodfin, L. (2014). *Leaders of their own learning: Transforming schools through student-engaged assessment*. San Francisco: Jossey-Bass.

Binder, M., & Freytag, A. (2013). Volunteering, subjective well-being and public policy. *Journal of Economic Psychology*, *34*, 97–119. https://doi.org/10.1016/j.joep.2012.11.008

Binfet, J.-T. (2022). *Cultivating kindness: An educator's guide*. Toronto, Ontario, Canada: University of Toronto Press.

Binfet, J.-T., Gadermann, A. M., & Schonert-Reichl, K. A. (2016). Measuring kindness at school: Psychometric properties of a school kindness scale for children and adolescents. *Psychology in the Schools*, *53*(2), 111–126. https://doi.org/10.1002/pits.21889

Birbal, R., Hewitt-Bradshaw, I., & James, F. (2023). Student voice as inclusive curricular practice in a technology course. *Caribbean Curriculum*, *29*, 165–186.

Blankstein, A. M., & Noguera, P. (2015). *Excellence through equity: Five principles of courageous leadership to guide achievement for every student*. Thousand Oaks, CA: Corwin.

Bock, L. (2015). *Work rules! Insights from inside Google that will transform how you live and lead*. New York: Twelve.

Boyes-Watson, C., & Pranis, K. (2015). *Circle forward: Building a restorative school community*. St. Paul, MN: Living Justice Press.

Bradshaw, A. C. (2018). Reconsidering the instructional design and technology timeline through a lens of social justice. *TechTrends*, *62*(4), 336–344. https://doi.org/10.1007/s11528-018-0269-6

Branch, N. A. (2019). Illuminating social justice in the framework: Transformative methodology, concept mapping, and learning outcomes development for critical information literacy. *Communications in Information Literacy*, *13*(1), 4–22. https://doi.org/10.15760/comminfolit.2019.13.1.2

Brown, B. (2017). *Braving the wilderness: The quest for true belonging and the courage to stand alone*. New York: Random House.

Brown, B. (2018). *Dare to lead: Brave work. Tough conversations. Whole hearts.* New York: Random House.

Camp, H. (2017). Goal setting as teacher development practice. *International Journal of Teaching and Learning in Higher Education, 29*(1), 61–72.

Cancialosi, C. (2017, May 30). *Preserving a culture people love as your company grows: Lessons from Zappos.* Accessed at www.forbes.com/sites/chriscancialosi/2017/05/30/preserving-a-culture-people-love-as-your-company-grows-lessons-from-zappos/?sh=3a03125f712b on February 29, 2024.

Carmeli, A., & Gittell, J. H. (2009). High-quality relationships, psychological safety, and learning from failures in work organizations. *Journal of Organizational Behavior, 30*(6), 709–729. https://doi.org/10.1002/job.565

Carnahan, B. (2023, May 25). *6 best practices for creating an inclusive and equitable interview process.* Accessed at www.hbs.edu/recruiting/insights-and-advice/blog/post/6-best-practices-to-creating-inclusive-and-equitable-interview-processes on March 1, 2024.

Carrington, J. (2020). *Kids these days: A game plan for (re)connecting with those we teach, lead, and love.* San Diego, CA: IMPress.

Carrington, J. (2023). *Feeling seen: Reconnecting in a disconnected world.* New York: Collins.

Casas, J. (2017). *Culturize: Every student. Every day. Whatever it takes.* San Diego, CA: Burgess.

Catmull, E. (2014). *Creativity, Inc.: Overcoming the unseen forces that stand in the way of true inspiration.* New York: Random House.

Chandler-Ward, J., Denevi, E., & Talusan, L. (Hosts). (2017). *Teaching while White* [Audio podcast]. Accessed at www.teachingwhilewhite.org/podcast on March 4, 2024.

Chellathurai, K. G. J. (2020). Future of education post pandemic COVID-19: Online vs classroom learning—Redefining education. *The Researchers' International Research Journal, 6*(2), 23–30.

Chicago Public Schools. (n.d.). *Office of Student Protections and Title IX.* Accessed at www.cps.edu/about/departments/office-of-student-protections-and-title-ix on November 6, 2023.

Chron. (2014, January 28). *UH-Clear Lake to observe Black History Month.* Accessed at www.chron.com/neighborhood/bayarea/news/article/uh-clear-lake-to-observe-black-history-month-5182198.php on November 6, 2023.

Coetzee, T., Pryce-Jones, K., Grant, L., & Tindle, R. (2022). Hope moderates the relationship between students' sense of belonging and academic misconduct. *International Journal for Educational Integrity, 18*(28). https://doi.org/10.1007/s40979-022-00121-0

Cole, C., & Mross, E. (2022). Ensuring more inclusive hiring processes. *Portal: Libraries and the Academy, 22*(3), 507–515. https://doi.org/10.1353/pla.2022.0037

Collins, J., & Hansen, M. T. (2011). *Great by choice: Uncertainty, chaos, and luck—Why some thrive despite them all.* New York: Harper Business.

Colvin, G., & Sugai, G. (2018). *Seven steps for developing a proactive schoolwide discipline plan: A guide for principals and leadership teams* (2nd ed.). Thousand Oaks, CA: Corwin.

Costello, B., Wachtel, J., & Wachtel, T. (2009). *The restorative practices handbook for teachers, disciplinarians, and administrators.* Bethlehem, PA: International Institute for Restorative Practices.

Coyle, D. (2018). *The culture code: The secrets of highly successful groups.* New York: Bantam Books.

Daimler, M. (2018, May 11). *Why great employees leave "great cultures."* Accessed at https://hbr.org/2018/05/why-great-employees-leave-great-cultures on November 7, 2023.

Darling-Hammond, L. (2010). *The flat world and education: How America's commitment to equity will determine our future.* New York: Teachers College Press.

Deci, E. L., & Ryan, R. M. (2000). The "what" and "why" of goal pursuits: Human needs and the self-determination of behavior. *Psychological Inquiry, 11*(4), 227–268.

Demmert, W. G., Jr. (2001). *Improving academic performance among Native American students: A review of the research literature.* Charleston, WV: ERIC Clearinghouse on Rural Education and Small Schools. Accessed at https://files.eric.ed.gov/fulltext/ED463917.pdf on November 6, 2023.

De Smet, A., Rubenstein, K., Schrah, G., Vierow, M., & Edmondson, A. (2021, February 11). *Psychological safety and the critical role of leadership development.* Accessed at www.mckinsey.com/capabilities/people-and-organizational-performance/our-insights/psychological-safety-and-the-critical-role-of-leadership-development on November 7, 2023.

Detert, J. R., & Edmondson, A. C. (2011). Implicit voice theories: Taken-for-granted rules of self-censorship at work. *Academy of Management Journal, 54*(3), 461–488.

DiAngelo, R. (2018). *White fragility: Why it's so hard for White people to talk about racism.* Boston: Beacon Press.

Dobbin, F., & Kalev, A. (2016). Why diversity programs fail. *Harvard Business Review, 94*(7), 52–60.

Dunbar, M. (2020). *Morning meetings and closing circles: Classroom-ready activities that increase student engagement and create a positive learning community.* Berkeley, CA: Ulysses Press.

Durlak, J. A., Weissberg, R. P., Dymnicki, A. B., Taylor, R. D., & Schellinger, K. B. (2011). The impact of enhancing students' social and emotional learning: A meta-analysis of school-based universal interventions. *Child Development, 82*(1), 405–432.

Dweck, C. S. (2016). *Mindset: The new psychology of success* (Updated ed.). New York: Random House.

Edmondson, A. C. (1999). Psychological safety and learning behavior in work teams. *Administrative Science Quarterly, 44*(2), 350–383. https:/doi.org/10.2307/2666999

Edmondson, A. C. (2019). *The fearless organization: Creating psychological safety in the workplace for learning, innovation, and growth.* Hoboken, NJ: Wiley.

Elgart, M. A. (2016). Creating state accountability systems that help schools improve. *Phi Delta Kappan, 98*(1), 26–30. https://doi.org/10.1177/0031721716666050

Enkel, E., & Bader, K. (2016). Why do experts contribute in cross-industry innovation? A structural model of motivational factors, intention and behavior. *R & D Management, 46*(S1), 207–226. https://doi.org/10.1111/radm.12132

Ferriss, T. (2009). *The 4-hour workweek: Escape 9–5, live anywhere, and join the new rich* (Expanded and updated ed., 1st rev. ed.). New York: Crown.

Follestad, B., & Wroldsen, N. (2019). *Using restorative circles in schools: How to build strong learning communities and foster student wellbeing.* London: Kingsley.

Foulk, T., Woolum, A., & Erez, A. (2016). Catching rudeness is like catching a cold: The contagion effects of low-intensity negative behaviors. *Journal of Applied Psychology, 101*(1), 50–67. https://doi.org/10.1037/apl0000037

Furrer, C., & Skinner, E. (2003). Sense of relatedness as a factor in children's academic engagement and performance. *Journal of Educational Psychology, 95*(1), 148–162.

Gaete, J., Rojas-Barahona, C. A., Olivares, E., & Araya, R. (2016). Brief report: Association between psychological sense of school membership and mental health among early adolescents. *Journal of Adolescence, 50*(1), 1–5. https://doi.org/10.1016/j.adolescence.2016.04.002

Gallagher, L. (2017). *The Airbnb story: How three ordinary guys disrupted an industry, made billions . . . and created plenty of controversy.* Boston: Houghton Mifflin Harcourt.

Garvin, D. A. (2013, December). *How Google sold its engineers on management.* Accessed at https://hbr.org/2013/12/how-google-sold-its-engineers-on-management on November 7, 2023.

Gates, R. M. (2014). *Duty: Memoirs of a secretary at war.* New York: Knopf.

Gay, G. (2018). *Culturally responsive teaching: Theory, research, and practice* (3rd ed.). New York: Teachers College Press.

Geher, G., Betancourt, K., & Jewell, O. (2017). The link between emotional intelligence and creativity. *Imagination, Cognition and Personality, 37*(1), 5–22.

Gelles, D. (2022). *Billionaire no more: Patagonia founder gives away the company.* Accessed at www.wku.edu/english/hs-writing-contest/hs-writing-contest23-composition.pdf on March 3, 2024.

Giroux, H. A. (2021). *Race, politics, and pandemic pedagogy: Education in a time of crisis.* London: Bloomsbury.

González, T., & Buth, A. J. (2019). Restorative justice at the crossroads: Politics, power, and language. *Contemporary Justice Review, 22*(3), 242–256. https://doi.org/10.1080/10282580.2019.1644172

Grant, A. (2013). *Give and take: Why helping others drives our success.* New York: Penguin Books.

Grant, A. M., & Berry, J. W. (2011). The necessity of others is the mother of invention: Intrinsic and prosocial motivations, perspective taking, and creativity. *Academy of Management Journal, 54*(1), 73–96.

Greene, R. J. (2019). *Rewarding performance: Guiding principles; custom strategies.* New York: Taylor & Francis.

Gregory, A., Clawson, K., Davis, A., & Gerewitz, J. (2016). The promise of restorative practices to transform teacher-student relationships and achieve equity in school discipline. *Journal of Educational and Psychological Consultation, 26*(4), 325–353. https://doi.org/10.1080/10474412.2014.929950

Gumz, E. J., & Grant, C. L. (2009). Restorative justice: A systematic review of the social work literature. *Families in Society, 90*(1), 119–126. https://doi.org/10.1606/1044-3894.3853

Hammond, Z. (2015). *Culturally responsive teaching and the brain: Promoting authentic engagement and rigor among culturally and linguistically diverse students.* Thousand Oaks, CA: Corwin.

Harris, K. (2003). *'Keep your distance': Remote communication, face-to-face, and the nature of community.* Accessed at www.local-level.org.uk/uploads/8/2/1/0/8210988/keep_your_distance_proofs.pdf on March 4, 2024.

Hattie, J. A. C. (2009). *Visible learning: A synthesis of over 800 meta-analyses relating to achievement.* New York: Routledge.

Henderson, A. T., & Mapp, K. L. (2002). *A new wave of evidence: The impact of school, family, and community connections on student achievement.* Austin, TX: Southwest Educational Development Laboratory.

Hoffman, R., Casnocha, B., & Yeh, C. (2014). *The alliance: Managing talent in the networked age.* Boston: Harvard Business Review Press.

Hsieh, T. (2010). *Delivering happiness: A path to profits, passion, and purpose.* New York: Grand Central.

Hurtado, S., Alvarez, C. L., Guillermo-Wann, C., Cuellar, M., & Arellano, L. (2012). A model for diverse learning environments: The scholarship on creating and assessing conditions for student success. In J. C. Smart & M. B. Paulsen (Eds.), *Higher education: Handbook of theory and research* (Vol. 27, pp. 41–122). Dordrecht, Netherlands: Springer. https://doi.org/10.1007/978-94-007-2950-6_2

International Institute for Restorative Practices. (n.d.). *Restorative practices.* Accessed at www.iirp.edu/images/pdf/Circles.pdf on November 7, 2023.

Jaiswal, S., & Prasad, C. (2020). Psycho-social factors influence family environment of secondary school students. *International Journal of Professional Studies, 10*, 47–52. Accessed at https://ijps.in/admin1/upload/04%20Shalini%20Jaiswal%2001158.pdf on February 22, 2024.

James, C., & Turner, T. (2017). *Towards race equity in education: The schooling of Black students in the Greater Toronto Area.* Toronto, Ontario, Canada: York University.

Jefferson Middle School. (n.d.). *2023 battle of the books.* Accessed at https://jefferson.apsva.us/battle-books-2022 on November 7, 2023.

Johnson, C. L., Alvarez, N. A., Hughes, J. A., McQuade, B. M., & Fuentes, D. G. (2024). Why we need to pay attention to stereotype threat. *American Journal of Pharmaceutical Education, 88*(4). https://doi.org/10.1016/j.ajpe.2024.100669

Kaçar, T., Terzi, R., Arıkan, İ., & Kırıkçı, A. C. (2021). The effect of inquiry-based learning on academic success: A meta-analysis study. *International Journal of Education and Literacy Studies, 9*(2), 15–23. https://doi.org/10.7575/aiac.ijels.v.9n.2p.15

Kanold, T. D., & Boogren, T. H. (2022). *Educator wellness: A guide for sustaining physical, mental, emotional, and social well-being.* Bloomington, IN: Solution Tree Press.

Kates, B. J. (1992). *We're different, we're the same.* New York: Random House.

Kena, G., Hussar, W., McFarland, J., de Brey, C., Musu-Gillette, L., Wang, X., et al. (2016). *The condition of education 2016.* Washinton, DC: U.S. Department of Education. Accessed at https://nces.ed.gov/pubs2016/2016144.pdf on November 7, 2023.

Kendi, I. X. (2019). *How to be an antiracist.* New York: One World.

Kervick, C. T., Moore, M., Ballysingh, T. A., Garnett, B. R., & Smith, L. C. (2019). The emerging promise of restorative practices to reduce discipline disparities affecting youth with disabilities and youth of color: Addressing access and equity. *Harvard Educational Review, 89*(4), 588–610. https://doi.org/10.17763/1943-5045-89.4.588

Kim, K., & Baker, M. A. (2017). How the employee looks and looks at you: Building customer-employee rapport. *Journal of Hospitality and Tourism Research, 43*(1), 20–40. https://doi.org/10.1177/1096348017731130

Kosciw, J. G., Greytak, E. A., Bartkiewicz, M. J., Boesen, M. J., & Palmer, N. A. (2012). *The 2011 National School Climate Survey: The experiences of lesbian, gay, bisexual and transgender youth in our nation's schools.* New York: Gay, Lesbian and Straight Education Network.

Ladson-Billings, G. (2014). Culturally relevant pedagogy 2.0: A.k.a. the remix. *Harvard Educational Review, 84*(1), 74–84. https://doi.org/10.17763/haer.84.1.p2rj131485484751

Lai, C. K., Marini, M., Lehr, S. A., Cerruti, C., Shin, J. E., Joy-Gaba. J. A., et al. (2014). Reducing implicit racial preferences: I. A comparative investigation of 17 interventions. *Journal of Experimental Psychology: General, 143*(4),1765–1785. https://doi.org/10.1037/a0036260

Layous, K., Nelson, S. K., Oberle, E., Schonert-Reichl, K. A., & Lyubomirsky, S. (2012). Kindness counts: Prompting prosocial behavior in preadolescents boosts peer acceptance and well-being. *PLOS ONE, 7*(12), e51380. https://doi.org/10.1371/journal.pone.0051380

MacKenzie, T. (2018). *Inquiry mindset: Nurturing the dreams, wonders, and curiosities of our youngest learners.* Irvine, CA: EdTechTeam Press.

Maimon, M. R., Howansky, K., & Sanchez, D. T. (2023). Fostering inclusivity: Exploring the impact of identity safety cues and instructor gender on students' impressions and belonging. *Teaching of Psychology, 50*(2), 105–111. https://doi.org/10.1177/00986283211043779

Mantchev, L. (2015). *Strictly no elephants.* New York: Simon & Schuster.

Marder, I. D., & Kurz, K. (2023). Micah E. Johnson and Jeffrey Weisberg, The little book of police youth dialogue: A restorative path toward justice [Book review]. *The International Journal of Restorative Justice, 6*(1), 165–168.

Mayworm, A. M., Sharkey, J. D., Hunnicutt, K. L., & Schiedel, K. C. (2016). Teacher consultation to enhance implementation of school-based restorative justice. *Journal of Educational and Psychological Consultation, 26*(4), 385–412.

McCluskey, G., Lloyd, G., Stead, J., Kane, J., Riddell, S., & Weedon, E. (2008). "I was dead restorative today": From restorative justice to restorative approaches in school. *Cambridge Journal of Education, 38*(2), 199–216.

McIntosh, P. (1989). *White privilege: Unpacking the invisible knapsack.* Accessed at www.nationalseedproject.org/key-seed-texts/white-privilege-unpacking-the-invisible-knapsack on March 22, 2024.

McQueen, N. (2015, July 29). *InDay: Investing in our employees so they can invest in themselves.* Accessed at www.linkedin.com/blog/member/career/inday-investing-in-our-employees-so-they-can-invest-in-themselves on March 14, 2024.

Michael, M. (Host). (2018, July 15). #1: The one thing this principal did daily to transform the most violent and dangerous school in Philadelphia (with Principal Linda Cliatt-Wayman) [Audio podcast episode]. In *KindSight 101.* Accessed at https://podcasts.apple.com/ca/podcast/1-the-one-thing-this-principal-did-daily-to-transform/id1412489005?i=1000415848176 on November 7, 2023.

Michael, M. (2022). *From burnt out to fired up: Reigniting your passion for teaching.* Bloomington, IN: Solution Tree Press.

Mitra, D. (2006). Increasing student voice and moving toward youth leadership. *Prevention Researcher, 13*(1), 7–10.

Moore, E., Jr., Michael, A., & Penick-Parks, M. W. (2018). *The guide for White women who teach Black boys.* Thousand Oaks, CA: Corwin.

Morrison, B. (2007). *Restoring safe school communities: A whole school response to bullying, violence and alienation.* Sydney, New South Wales, Australia: Federation Press.

Moss-Racusin, C. A., Dovidio, J. F., Brescoll, V. L., Graham, M. J., & Handelsman, J. (2012). Science faculty's subtle gender biases favor male students. *Proceedings of the National Academy of Sciences, 109*(41), 16474–16479. https://doi.org/10.1073/pnas.1211286109

Murphy, M. C., & Zirkel, S. (2015). Race and belonging in school: How anticipated and experienced belonging affect choice, persistence, and performance. *Teachers College Record*, *117*(12), 1–40. https://doi.org/10.1177/016146811511701204

Murphy, S. (2019). *Fostering mindfulness: Building skills that students need to manage their attention, emotions, and behavior in classrooms and beyond*. Markham, Ontario, Canada: Pembroke.

National Education Association Center for Social Justice. (2021, June). *NEA LGBTQ+ resources*. Accessed at www.nea.org/resource-library/nea-lgbtq-resources on November 7, 2023.

National School Climate Center. (n.d.). *School climate survey*. Accessed at www.school climate.org/climate on November 7, 2023.

Newkirk, P. (2019). *Diversity, Inc.: The failed promise of a billion-dollar business*. New York: Bold Type Books.

Okun, T. (2010). *The emperor has no clothes: Teaching about race and racism to people who don't want to know*. Charlotte, NC: Information Age.

Osterman, K. F. (2000). Students' need for belonging in the school community. *Review of Educational Research*, *70*(3), 323–367.

Parham, W. D. (2014). *Journal of Multicultural Counseling and Development*: Second special issue on diversity and inclusion in higher education. *Journal of Multicultural Counseling and Development*, *42*(3), 130–131. https://doi.org/10.1002/j.2161-1912.2014.00049.x

Paumgarten, N. (2016, September 12). *Patagonia's philosopher-king*. Accessed at www.newyorker.com/magazine/2016/09/19/patagonias-philosopher-king on November 7, 2023.

Pavelka, S. (2013). Practices and policies for implementing restorative justice within schools. *Prevention Researcher*, *20*(1), 15–17.

Payne, A. A., & Welch, K. (2015). Restorative justice in schools: The influence of race on restorative discipline. *Youth & Society*, *47*(4), 539–564. https://doi.org/10.1177/0044118X12473125

Penfold, A. (2018). *All are welcome*. New York: Knopf.

Pollock, M. (2017). *Schooltalk: Rethinking what we say about—and to—students every day*. New York: The New Press.

Pons, F., Harris, P. L., & Doudin, P.-A. (2002). Teaching emotion understanding. *European Journal of Psychology of Education*, *17*(3), 293–304.

Porath, C. (2016). *Mastering civility: A manifesto for the workplace*. New York: Grand Central.

Porath, C. (2018). *Why being respectful to your coworkers is good for business* [Video file]. TED Conferenccs. Accessed at www.ted.com/talks/christine_porath_why_being_nice_to_your_coworkers_is_good_for_business on November 7, 2023.

Pranis, K. (2005). *The little book of circle processes: A new/old approach to peacemaking.* Intercourse, PA: Good Books.

Prilleltensky, I. (2005). Promoting well-being: Time for a paradigm shift in health and human services. *Scandinavian Journal of Public Health, 33*(Suppl. 66), 53–60.

Project Implicit. (n.d.). *Preliminary information.* Accessed at https://implicit.harvard.edu/implicit/takeatest.html on November 7, 2023.

Rands, M. L., & Gansemer-Topf, A. M. (2017). The room itself is active: How classroom design impacts student engagement. *Journal of Learning Spaces, 6*(1), 26–33.

Rao, K., Ok, M. W., & Bryant, B. R. (2014). A review of research on universal design educational models. *Remedial and Special Education, 35*(3), 153–166.

Reichenbach, L. (2022, September 15). *Edmonds school board hears reports on career and technical education, student discipline plan.* Accessed at https://myedmondsnews.com/2022/09/edmonds-school-board-hears-reports-on-career-and-technical-education-student-discipline-plan on November 7, 2023.

Rivera, J. (2024). *Culturally responsive teaching and learning achievement* [Doctoral dissertation, Seattle Pacific University]. Digital Commons @ SPU. https://digitalcommons.spu.edu/soe_etd/80

Rolland, R. (2022). *The art of talking with children: The simple keys to nurturing kindness, creativity, and confidence in kids.* New York: HarperOne.

Rose, T. (2022). *Collective illusions: Conformity, complicity, and the science of why we make bad decisions.* New York: Hachette Books.

Ruthig, J. C., Haynes, T. L., Stupnisky, R. H., & Perry, R. P. (2009). Perceived academic control: Mediating the effects of optimism and social support on college students' psychological health. *Social Psychology of Education, 12*(2), 233–249. https://doi.org/10.1007/s11218-008-9079-6

Sandberg, S. (2013). *Lean in: Women, work, and the will to lead.* New York: Knopf.

Schultz, H. (2011). *Onward: How Starbucks fought for its life without losing its soul.* New York: Rodale.

Scott, K. (2017). *Radical candor: Be a kick-ass boss without losing your humanity.* New York: St. Martin's Press.

Singleton, G. E., & Linton, C. (2006). *Courageous conversations about race: A field guide for achieving equity in schools.* Thousand Oaks, CA: Corwin.

Smith, W., & Lewis, M. (2022). *Both/and thinking: Embracing creative tensions to solve your toughest problems.* Boston: Harvard Business Review Press.

Spencer, S. J., Logel, C., & Davies, P. G. (2016). Stereotype threat. *Annual Review of Psychology, 67,* 415–437. https://doi.org/10.1146/annurev-psych-073115-103235

Stanier, M. B. (2016). *The coaching habit: Say less, ask more & change the way you lead forever.* Toronto, Ontario, Canada: Box of Crayons Press.

Sue, D. W. (2015). *Race talk and the conspiracy of silence: Understanding and facilitating difficult dialogues on race*. Hoboken, NJ: Wiley.

Suh, E. M. (2002). Culture, identity consistency, and subjective well-being. *Journal of Personality and Social Psychology*, *83*(6), 1378–1391. https://doi.org/10.1037/0022-3514.83.6.1378

Sukhera, J., & Watling, C. (2018). A framework for integrating implicit bias recognition into health professions education. *Academic Medicine*, *93*(1), 35–40.

Sullivan, S. (2018). Becoming a citizen: Habits of national belonging in the United States. *Geografiska Annaler*, *100*(2), 163–177. https://doi.org/10.1080/04353684.2017.1401904

Talapatra, J. (2022). Environmental leadership—Case studies. In T. Sharma, R. Sinha Ray, & N. Mitra (Eds.), *Responsible leadership for sustainability in uncertain times: Social, economic and environmental challenges for sustainable organizations* (pp. 281–296). Singapore: Springer. https://doi.org/10.1007/978-981-19-4723-0_16

Tan, R., Schwab, S., & Perren, S. (2022). Teachers' beliefs about peer social interactions and their relationship to practice in Chinese inclusive preschools. *International Journal of Early Years Education*, *30*(2), 463–477. https://doi.org/10.1080/09669760.2021.1983775

Tatum, B. D. (1997). *Why are all the Black kids sitting together in the cafeteria? And other conversations about race*. New York: Basic Books.

Tatum, B. D. (2017). "Why are all the Black kids still sitting together in the cafeteria?" And other conversations about race in the twenty-first century. *Liberal Education*, *103*(3–4), 46–55.

Taylor, C., & Peter, T. (2011). *Every class in every school: The first national climate survey on homophobia, biphobia, and transphobia in Canadian schools*. Toronto, Ontario, Canada: Egale Canada Human Rights Trust. Accessed at https://egale.ca/wp-content/uploads/2011/05/Every-Class-In-Every-School-Final-Report.pdf on November 7, 2023.

Thorsborne, M., & Blood, P. (2013). *Implementing restorative practices in schools: A practical guide to transforming school communities*. London: Kingsley.

Torkelson, E., Holm, K., Bäckström, M., & Schad, E. (2016). Factors contributing to the perpetuation of workplace incivility: The importance of organizational aspects and experiencing incivility from others. *Work & Stress*, *30*(2), 115–131. https://doi.org/10.1080/02678373.2016.1175524

Tyler, M. (2005). *The skin you live in*. Chicago: Chicago Children's Museum.

U.S. Department of Education. (2016, October 28). *2013–2014 civil rights data collection: A first look*. Accessed at www2.ed.gov/about/offices/list/ocr/docs/2013-14-first-look.pdf on November 7, 2023.

Van Ness, D. W., & Strong, K. H. (2014). *Restoring justice* (5th ed.). New York: Routledge.

Vides Saade, M., & Halder, D. (Eds.). (2023). *Minding the gap between restorative justice, therapeutic jurisprudence, and global Indigenous wisdom*. Hershey, PA: IGI Global.

Waber, B., Magnolfi, J., & Lindsay, G. (2014, October). *Workspaces that move people.* Accessed at https://hbr.org/2014/10/workspaces-that-move-people on November 7, 2023.

Wachtel, T. (2016). *Defining restorative.* Accessed at www.iirp.edu/images/pdf/Defining-Restorative_Nov-2016.pdf on November 7, 2023.

Walton, G. M., & Cohen, G. L. (2011). A brief social-belonging intervention improves academic and health outcomes of minority students. *Science, 331*(6023), 1447–1451. https://doi.org/10.1126/science.1198364

Wang, M.-T., & Peck, S. C. (2013). Adolescent educational success and mental health vary across school engagement profiles. *Developmental Psychology, 49*(7), 1266–1276.

Washington and Lee University. (n.d.). *Student organizations.* Accessed at https://my.wlu.edu/office-of-inclusion-and-engagement/diversity-resources/student-organizations on November 7, 2023.

Westwood, L. (2023, December 22). *Salesforce 1-1-1 model: Understanding the impact of the pledge 1% initiative.* Accessed at www.salesforceben.com/salesforce-1-1-1-model-understanding-the-impact-of-the-pledge-1-initiative on June 6, 2024.

Wolf, K. C., & Kupchik, A. (2017). School suspensions and adverse experiences in adulthood. *Justice Quarterly, 34*(3), 407–430. https://doi.org/10.1080/07418825.2016.1168475

Woodson, J. (2018). *The day you begin.* New York: Paulsen.

Woolford, A., & Nelund, A. (2019). *The politics of restorative justice: A critical introduction* (2nd ed.). Black Point, Nova Scotia, Canada: Fernwood.

Workhuman. (2017, November 2). *New Globoforce survey finds frequent check-ins, values-based recognition help employees find greater meaning in their work.* Accessed at https://press.workhuman.com/press-releases/globoforce-recognition-employees on May 20, 2024.

Zachary, L. J. (2009). *The mentee's guide: Making mentoring work for you.* San Francisco: Jossey-Bass.

Zaidi, S. (2022). Integrating psychological safety: Using the all-in method to cultivate belonging and understanding in diversity and inclusion. *AI Practitioner, 24,* 37–42.

Zehr, H. (2015). *The little book of restorative justice* (Rev. and updated). New York: Good Books.

INDEX

A

academic outcomes and belonging, 6
accessibility, 84
accountability
    bias and, 90–91
    restorative justice practices and, 123
achievement walls, 67
active listening, 28, 56, 62. *See also* listening
affirmations
    belonging affirmations, 69
    belonging cues and, 56, 63
    icebreaker activities, 134
Allen curve, 53
anti-bias workshop series, 101
anti-bullying policies and programs, 84
appreciation events, 50
attendance and belonging, 6
audio and digital books, 99
augmentative and alternative communication (AAC) devices, 99
awards, 50, 67
AWE questions, 32

B

"Becoming a Citizen: Habits of National Belonging in the United States" (Sullivan), 126
belonging
    about, 16–18
    for adults, 10
    challenges of building a belonging culture in schools, 7–10
    classroom toolbox for building a culture of belonging, 24–29
    designing your blueprint: laying the foundation for belonging, 37
    environments of belonging, 2–5
    focusing on belonging to yourself first, 18
    impact of on students, 6–7
    reproducibles for, 38
    school leadership toolbox for building a culture of belonging, 30–35
    in schools, 5–7, 22–23
    strategies for building belonging as educators and school leaders, 19–22
    vignettes for, 1–2, 7, 8, 9, 15–16, 22, 32
belonging cues
    fostering generosity, kindness, and empathy, 55–56
    strategies to build community using, 62–63
belonging rituals, 69
bias exploration: dismantling implicit bias in schools. *See* implicit bias
bias training, 90. *See also* implicit bias
bias-free hiring, 115–116. *See also* implicit bias
bingo icebreakers, 133
blind drawing, 133
body language, 56, 62, 63
book clubs
    antiracism book and film club, 101
    multicultural book clubs, 100
both/and thinking, 111
boundaries. *See also* BUILD framework
    about, 12
    cultivating creative tension, 145
    five key questions: inclusive classroom resource filter, 97–98
    givers and, 47
    parent and community engagement, 144–145
    professional development, 143–144
    psychological safety in the classroom, 24–25
    starting with school culture, 30
Braving the Wilderness (Brown), 18
breaking the code game, 133
Brown, B., 18
buddy programs, 33–34
BUILD framework, 4–5, 12–13. *See also specific elements of*
building a culture of belonging. *See* belonging
bullying and aggression, 6, 84
Burnaby School District, Burnaby, British Columbia, 93

C

challenge
    focus challenge, 31
    seeing challenges, not failures, 68–69
charades, 133
Chicago Public Schools Office of Student Protections and Title IX, 94–96
choice
    choice boards, 74
    choice in assignments, 27
    empowering with student voice and choice, 26–28
circle processes, 138–141
class murals, 133
class talent shows, 133
classroom environment
    inclusive classroom resource filter, 97–98
    inclusive school culture and, 84
    kindness and, 44–45
    safe environments and, 88–91
    strategies to build proximity and foster belonging through classroom design, 54–55
    tech tips for, 99
classroom toolboxes
    building a culture of belonging, 24–29
    dismantling implicit bias in schools, 97–108
    fostering generosity, kindness, and empathy, 59–69
    restorative justice practices, 131–141
clothing donation drives, 60–61
coding club for all skill levels, 100
collaboration
    collaborative decision making, 27
    teamwork and collaboration, 10
communication
    augmentative and alternative communication (AAC) devices, 99
    challenges of building a belonging culture in schools, 9
    culturally responsive leadership and, 114–115
    proximity and, 53–55
    recognizing teachers and, 50
    restorative justice practices and, 123, 127–128
    strategic questioning and, 75
    transparent communication, 73

163

community and family
    belonging and, 6
    diversity and inclusion partnerships with community organizers, 102–103
    inclusive school culture and, 84
    parent and community engagement, 144–145
    restorative justice practices and, 124
community clean-up events, 60
community connection circles, 132–135
compassion practice, 132
compliments
    activities for a kinder classroom, 59–60
    compliment circles, 65–66
    icebreaker activities, 133
    types of, 66
creativity
    belonging and, 10
    cultivating creative tension, 145
cultural appreciation, 88
cultural appropriation, 88
culturally responsive practices
    case studies of inclusive and diverse schools and, 91–96
    challenges of building a belonging culture in schools, 8
    culturally responsive leadership, 114–115
    inclusive school culture and, 83
    power and privilege and, 9
culture, prioritizing over academics, 5
culture videos, 34–35
cultures of belonging. See belonging
curricular design
    accountability and bias and, 91
    case studies of inclusive and diverse schools and, 91–96
    inclusive school culture and, 84

D

decision making
    belonging and, 10
    collaborative decision making, 27
delegating and school leadership, 72, 75
dependability. See also BUILD framework
    about, 13
    activities for a kinder classroom, 59–60
    belonging affirmations, 69
    bias-free hiring, 115–116
    bridging perspectives, 111–112
    celebrating the wins, 67
    compliment circles, 65–66
    cultivating creative tension, 145
    culturally responsive leadership, 114–115
    diversity and inclusion partnerships with community organizers, 102–103
    generosity or gratitude journals, 63–64
    morning meetings, 28–29
    new teacher and student onboarding, 33–35
    parent and community engagement, 144–145
    professional development, 143–144
    showing your gratitude, 70–71
    tech tips, 98–99
dismantling implicit bias in schools. See implicit bias

diversity
    bolstering diversity and inclusion, 89–90
    definitions of equity, diversity, and inclusion within the context of bias, 83
    diversity and inclusion partnerships with community organizers, 102–103
    inclusive school culture and, 84
    recommended resources to learn about, 86–87

E

egg drop challenge, 133
elderly or homebound individuals, support for, 61
emotions charades, 26
emotions circles, 26
empathy. See also fostering generosity, kindness, and empathy
    empathy workshops, 43
    leadership and, 44
    restorative justice practices and, 123
empowering with student voice and choice, 26–28
environmental clubs, 43, 101
environmental conservation projects, 61
equity
    case studies of inclusive and diverse schools and, 91–96
    definitions of equity, diversity, and inclusion within the context of bias, 83
    equity in action days, 42
events, local and virtual, 21
expectations
    psychological safety in the classroom, 24
    starting with school culture, 30
eye contact, 56, 62

F

failure
    fear of failure, 21
    seeing challenges, not failures, 68–69
feedback
    accountability and bias and, 91
    encouraging vulnerability, 72
    peer feedback and reflection, 27
    strategies to build community using belonging cues, 62
    zooming in on implicit bias with your team, 111
feelings journals, 26
fire-starter questions, 25–26
five key questions: inclusive classroom resource filter, 97–98
five strategies for building belonging as educators and school leaders, 19–22
focus challenge, 31
Follestad, B., 122
food drives, 60
forgiveness practice, 131–132
fostering generosity, kindness, and empathy
    about, 40–41
    belonging cues, 55–56
    belonging through proximity, 53–55
    classroom toolbox for, 59–69

conclusion, 76
contagion of incivility in schools, 51–53
giving styles, 45–48
kindness as a priority, 42–45
recognition gap, 48–50
reproducibles for, 77
school leadership toolbox for, 70–75
vignettes for, 39–40, 44, 45, 47
vulnerability cycle, 56–58
foundation: building a culture of belonging. See belonging
four corners on moral dilemmas, 133
four small words, 133
fruit salad game, 133
fundraising for educational initiatives, 61

G

genders and sexualities alliances (GSAs), 100
generosity. See also fostering generosity, kindness, and empathy
    fostering, 40–41
    generosity or gratitude journals, 63–64
    givers, 46, 47, 48
    giving styles, 45–48
    goals, establishing a shared purpose and goals, 73
graphic organizers, 99
gratitude
    gratitude practice, 131
    showing your gratitude, 70–71
group juggling, 133
growth mindsets, 68

H

happiness committees, 42
Harvey Milk High School, New York, New York, 92
High Tech High School, San Diego, California, 92
high-five train, 133
human knot, 134

I

"I" statements, 128
icebreaker activities, 132–135
identity maps, 113
Implicit Association Test (IAT), 86, 87, 88, 107
implicit bias
    about, 81–82
    case studies of inclusive and diverse schools, 91–96
    challenges of building a belonging culture in schools and, 7–8
    classroom toolbox for dismantling implicit bias, 97–108
    conclusion, 117
    definitions of equity, diversity, and inclusion within the context of bias, 82–85
    journal: self-reflection on implicit bias, 109
    meaning of bias, 85–87
    multigrade lessons for teaching about, 103–108
    recommended resources to learn about, 86–87
    reproducibles for, 118

Index

revealing implicit bias, 87–88
safe environments for all, 88–91
school leadership toolbox for dismantling implicit bias, 109–116
vignettes for, 79–80
zooming in on implicit bias with your team, 109–111
incivility, contagion of, 51–53. *See also* fostering generosity, kindness, and empathy
inclusion
    accountability and bias and, 91
    bolstering diversity and, 89–90
    definitions of equity, diversity, and inclusion within the context of bias, 83
    diversity and inclusion partnerships with community organizers, 102–103
        inclusive classroom resource filter, 97–98
    recommended resources to learn about, 86–87
Indian Community School, Franklin, Wisconsin, 93
individual professional learning plans (ILPs), 74
innovation time off, 43
inquiry-based learning, 61
integrity. *See also* BUILD framework
    about, 12
    activities for a kinder classroom, 59–60
    bias-free hiring, 115–116
    bridging perspectives, 111–112
    celebrating the wins, 67
    circle processes, 138–141
    compliment circles, 65–66
    cultivating creative tension, 145
    culturally responsive leadership, 114–115
    diversity and inclusion partnerships with community organizers, 102–103
    empowering with student voice and choice, 26–28
    encouraging vulnerability, 71–72
    five key questions: inclusive classroom resource filter, 97–98
    journal: self-reflection on implicit bias, 109
    mindful practices, 131–132
    parent and community engagement, 144–145
    peace corners, 136–137
    professional development, 143–144
    restorative staff meetings, 142–143
    service-learning projects, 60–61
    showing your gratitude, 70–71
    strategic questioning, 74–75
    strategies to build community using belonging cues, 62–63
    tech tips, 98–99
    zooming in on implicit bias with your team, 109–111
introduction
    about environments of belonging, 2–5
    belonging for adults, 10
    belonging in schools, importance of, 5–7
    challenges of building a belonging culture in schools, 7–10
    in this book, 11–13
    vignettes for, 1–2, 7, 8, 9

J
job satisfaction, 10
joke day, 134
journaling
    activities for a kinder classroom, 59–60
    challenge journals, 68
    feelings journal, 26
    generosity or gratitude journals, 63–64
    journal: self-reflection on implicit bias, 109

K
kindness. *See also* fostering generosity, kindness, and empathy
    activities for a kinder classroom, 59–60
    acts of kindness, 41, 48, 59, 75, 134
    as a priority, 42–45
    impact of, 41
    "kindness coins" reward system, 67

L
leaders, use of term, 3
leadership. *See also* school leadership toolboxes
    culturally responsive leadership, 114–115
    encouraging vulnerability, 71–72
    kindness and empathy and, 44
    personal ownership and, 3
    self-leadership, 17
listening. *See also* BUILD framework
    about, 12–13
    active listening, 28, 56, 62
    AWE questions and, 32
    circle process, 138–141
    community connection circles, 132–135
    empowering student-led special interest groups, 99–101
    peace corners, 136–137
    recognizing individual differences, 112–113
    restorative chats, 135–136
    restorative staff meetings, 142–143
    storytelling to focus on kindness and generosity, 64–65
    strategies to build community using belonging cues, 62–63

M
matchers, 46, 47. *See also* giving styles
meetings
    AWE questions and, 32
    bridging perspectives, 111–112
    contagion of incivility and, 52
    empowering student-led special interest groups, 99–100
    empowering with student voice and choice, 26, 27
    focus challenge and, 31
    morning meetings, 28–29
    recognition and, 48, 49
    restorative staff meetings, 142–143
    showing your gratitude, 70–71
mental health, 6, 10
mentorship
    activities for a kinder classroom, 59–60
    bolstering diversity and inclusion and, 89, 90
    buddy programs, 33–34
    school connections and, 71
microaggressions, 81
micro-credentialing, 74
mind mapping, 99
mindfulness
    mindfulness practices, 131–132
    zooming in on implicit bias with your team, 111
mirroring or mimicking, 56
mistake of the week, 68
modeling, 28
morning meetings, 28–29. *See also* meetings
motivation, 6
murals, 113, 133

N
new learning, 21
norms
    empowering student-led interest groups, 100
    morning meetings and, 28
    new teacher and student onboarding and, 33
    psychological safety in the classroom and, 24–25
    strategies to build proximity and foster belonging, 55
    vulnerability cycle and, 57

O
onboarding for new teachers and students, 33–35
online communities, 21

P
pair-and-share techniques, 62
paper towers, 134
paraprofessionals, recognizing, 49–50
parental involvement and belonging, 6
peace corners, 136–137
peers
    belonging affirmations and, 69
    celebrating the wins, 67
    peer feedback and reflection, 27
    peer-to-peer recognition, 70
    seeing challenges, not failures, 69
perspective taking, 90, 111–112, 145
positive affirmation cards, 134
positive name game, 134
positive school culture: fostering generosity, kindness, and empathy. *See* fostering generosity, kindness, and empathy
power and privilege, 9–10, 81
professional development
    on bias and inclusion, 83
    designing personalized professional learning, 73–74
        individual professional learning plans (ILPs), 74
    recognizing paraprofessionals, 49
    recognizing teachers, 50

restorative justice practices and, 143–144
safe environments for all and, 90
showing your gratitude, 70–71
zooming in on implicit bias with your team, 111
proximity, belonging through, 53–55
psychological safety
belonging and, 10
in the classroom, 24–25
safe environments for all, 89
purpose, establishing a shared purpose and goals, 73

Q

questions
AWE questions, 32
fire-starter questions, 25–26
five key questions: inclusive classroom resource filter, 97–98
strategic questioning, 74–75

R

recognition
celebrating the wins, 67
peer-to-peer recognition, 70
recognition gap, 48–50
recognizing individual differences, 112–113
reflection
circle processes, 138
feelings reflections, 26
journal: self-reflection on implicit bias, 109
multigrade lessons for teaching about implicit bias and, 105, 106, 108
peer feedback and, 27
professional development and, 144
seeing challenges, not failures and, 68
strategic questioning and, 75
strategies for building belonging as educators and school leaders, 19
zooming in on implicit bias with your team, 111
relay races, 134
reproducibles for
designing your blueprint: addressing implicit bias, 118
designing your blueprint: laying the foundation for belonging, 38
designing your blueprint: restorative justice and building relationships, 147
designing your blueprint: using kindness as a building block, 77
resilience, 6
resources
inclusive classroom resource filter, 97–98
restorative justice practices and, 129
strategies to build proximity and foster belonging, 54
respect, 123
restorative chats, 135–136
restorative justice practices
about, 121
classroom toolbox for, 131–141
communication and, 127–128
conclusion, 146
core principles of, 123–128
evaluation and continuous improvement of, 130
inclusive school culture and, 84
meaning of restorative justice, 121–122
obstacles to, 128–129
reproducibles for, 147
school leadership toolbox for, 142–145
school-to-prison pipeline and, 125–127
versus traditional discipline, 124–125
vignettes for, 119–121, 124–125
restorative staff meetings, 142–143
role models, 68
rudeness, 51

S

scavenger hunts, 134
school climate, 6
school culture, 30
school leadership toolboxes
building a culture of belonging, 30–35
dismantling implicit bias in schools, 109–116
fostering generosity, kindness, and empathy, 70–75
restorative justice practices, 142–145
school-to-prison pipeline and restorative justice, 125–127. See also restorative justice practices
screen readers, 99
seating arrangements, 44–45, 54
secret friends, 134
self-leadership, 17
service-learning projects, 60–61
silent lineups, 134
Skyline High School, Ann Arbor, Michigan, 94
smile pass, 134
social skills and belonging, 6
social-emotional learning (SEL)
case studies of inclusive and diverse schools and, 91–96
inclusive school culture and, 84–85
morning meetings and, 29
student success and, 44
special interest groups, 99–101
speech-to-text (STT) software, 98
Stanier, M., 31, 75
stereotype threat, 7–8, 85, 112
stigma, 85
stories
circle processes, 138
shared success stories, 50
storytelling to focus on kindness and generosity, 64–65
strategic questioning, 74–75
strategies for building belonging as educators and school leaders, 19–22
strength spotting, 69
student voice, 26–28, 84
student-led discussions, 27
student-led initiatives, 27
students with disabilities, support group for, 101
Sullivan, S., 126

T

takers, 46, 47. See also giving styles
teachers, recognizing, 50
team-building retreats, 43
teamwork and collaboration, 10
technology
teaching tech for a good cause, 42
tech tips, 98–99
Texas hug, 135
text-to-speech (TTS) software, 98
thank-you notes, 49
Toronto District School Board, Toronto, Ontario, 94
toxic behaviors, 51
traditional discipline versus restorative justice, 124–125. See also restorative justice practices
transparency
accountability and bias and, 91
transparent communication, 73
turn taking, 28
two truths and a lie, 135

U

understanding. See also BUILD framework
about, 12
belonging affirmations, 69
circle processes, 138–141
community connection circles, 132–135
designing personalized professional learning, 73–74
empowering student-led special interest groups, 99–101
feelings reflections, 26
fire-starter questions, 25–26
focus challenge, 31
journal: self-reflection on implicit bias, 109
multigrade lessons for teaching about implicit bias, 103–108
peace corners, 136–137
recognizing individual differences, 112–113
restorative chats, 135–136
restorative staff meetings, 142–143
storytelling to focus on kindness and generosity, 64–65
tech tips, 98–99
zooming in on implicit bias with your team, 109–111
Universal Design for Learning, 61

V

vision, 73
visual representations, 24
volunteer time off, 43
vulnerability
encouraging vulnerability, 71–72
vulnerability cycle, 56–58

W

walk a mile exercise, 110
welcome gifts, 35
welcome letters, 33
wins, celebrating, 67
Wroldsen, N., 122

Z

zero-tolerance policies, 126
zooming in on implicit bias with your team, 109–111

From Burnt Out to Fired Up
Morgane Michael
Overwhelmed teachers, this book is for you. The truth is that you can be remarkable without burning out. Drawing from the latest research and her own teaching experiences, author Morgane Michael delivers research-backed strategies to replenish your well-being and reignite your passion for your purpose.
BKG027

Raising Equity Through SEL
Jorge Valenzuela
Activate social-emotional learning effectively in your classroom with this trusted source for sound pedagogy that addresses the academic and SEL needs of diverse learners. Each strategy, tool, and template shared is meant to facilitate your practice by making SEL easier to implement.
BKG041

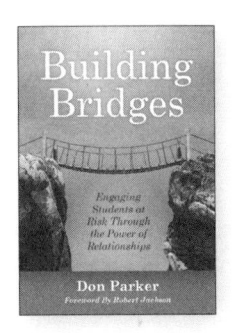

Building Bridges
Don Parker
Research shows that discipline problems are one of the greatest challenges in education. In *Building Bridges*, author Don Parker shows educators how to address this issue head-on, to build teacher-student relationships and create a welcoming learning environment that promotes engagement and achievement.
BKF846

Embracing Relational Teaching
Anthony R. Reibel
When you shift to relational pedagogy, you establish connections that help students feel valued, respected, and heard, which leads to enhanced student engagement. This book explores the relational approach and offers strategies to embed student-teacher relationships into everyday interactions and learning.
BKF949

Solution Tree | Press — a division of Solution Tree

Visit SolutionTree.com or call 800.733.6786 to order.

Wait! Your professional development journey doesn't have to end with the last pages of this book.

We realize improving student learning doesn't happen overnight. And your school or district shouldn't be left to puzzle out all the details of this process alone.

No matter where you are on the journey, we're committed to helping you get to the next stage.

Take advantage of everything from **custom workshops** to **keynote presentations** and **interactive web and video conferencing**. We can even help you develop an action plan tailored to fit your specific needs.

Let's get the conversation started.

Call 888.763.9045 today.

SolutionTree.com